T I

MW00930285

THEN WHAT?

LIFE AFTER JESUS SAVES

A Third Timothy™ Christian Living Book

Copyright © 2019 by Tim Leiphart

ISBN: 9781080240135

All rights reserved. No part of this book may be reproduced in any form without permission in writing from the publisher, except for brief quotations used in critical articles or reviews.

Unless otherwise indicated, all Scripture quotations are taken from the Holy Bible, New Living Translation, copyright 1996, 2004, 2007, 2015 by Tyndale House Foundation. Used by permission of Tyndale House Publishers, Inc., Carol Stream, Illinois 60188. All rights reserved.

Also read:

Ripening on the Vine: A 365-Day Devotional (2018)
Unlikely King: A Daily Devotional for Real People (2017)
The Next Day: How God Still Speaks (2011)

Connect online at www.thirdtimothy.com

"I will study your commandments and reflect on your ways." (Psalms 119:15)

CONTENTS

Introduction

Everyone has an element of spiritual curiosity that draws them to the unknown, to the supernatural. In Christian circles we understand this to be God calling humans to know their Creator, an invitation to begin a personal relationship with the one who gave them breath and a heartbeat. To this end, missionaries and evangelists and preachers and prophets throughout the ages have endeavored to introduce people to Jesus. It seems they must have had a fair amount of success since research indicates about one-third of the global population now claims Christianity as its religion.

But then what? How does it actually work? What should we do with the everyday problems that don't go away? Where do we turn when we have tough questions? Who can we count on to sincerely care and not laugh or ridicule or judge or ignore? When will we finally get the answers we need? Why is it so hard!

As you've probably already discovered, being a Christian is not easy and it's not always fun. The challenges to godly living are endless and there are so many ways to trip that sometimes you just want to stay home curled up in bed. But never fear: God saw this coming and he has the perfect word for every situation.

Meeting with a personal counselor is one of the most effective options, but it can take lots of time and lots of money to get to the bottom of some of the most difficult issues, and people don't generally have much of either to spare. There is now a quicker solution! This book includes a unique collection of real-life conversations taken from private online counseling sessions that benefited, surprisingly, from the advantages of distance and near-anonymity. Due to the added confidentiality provided to the participants, we've been able to cover some of the most sensitive and sometimes controversial topics; plus you will find the pages filled with the vulnerability and incredible honesty that comes with trust and confidence in God.

So get ready! It's unavoidable that your spirit will grow stronger and you will gain more peace for the journey as you open your heart and mind. "Let God transform you into a new person by changing the way you think. Then you will learn to know God's will for you, which is good and pleasing and perfect." (Romans 12:2)

Why does God allow pain and death?

Q: The young girl sits by a hospital bed watching her grandmother cling to life, supported by medicine and machines, sedated and unresponsive; prayers seem empty and hope is fleeting. Heartbroken and sobbing, she asks, "If God loves us, why would he let this happen?"

A: In one form or another this question is being asked all over the world. As Christians we are fond of saying that God is good, all the time. But it's times like this that bring us right up to the edge of our convictions; do we really believe it, do we really believe God is good? How then can God allow this, the pain and misery of death? I want to help you to shift your thinking: Physical death is a blessing from God.

In the very beginning God told Adam and Eve they could eat fruit from all of the trees in the garden, except from the tree of the knowledge of good and evil; "If you eat its fruit, you are sure to die." They both disobeyed and ate from the tree. Although death didn't come to them immediately, death did come. God had to kill an animal to provide skins to cover them, for their sin exposed their nakedness and they were ashamed. How can any of this be good?

Because of the next action by God: He banned Adam and Eve from the garden lest they also eat from the tree of life and live forever in their sinful state, guilty and ashamed. What died immediately was the relationship they had previously enjoyed with their Creator; no longer would they walk together in the cool of the evening, no more intimate conversations, no more innocence. Life as they knew it was over, death had raised its ugly head and it has been stalking us ever since.

But God's love for us is so all-encompassing that even our sin can't stop him. Our physical lives on earth have an end but his forgiveness offers us new bodies and a new life permanently in heaven with him. He is working now to transform our minds, to help us to understand his greater mission of healing and restoration. God does answer our prayers, God does heal— because he truly is good, all the time. It's his timing that we question as it doesn't always fit with our wishes.

We call God our Heavenly Father; compare his role to the ones we fill as earthly fathers and mothers and try to relate to the vast love he has for his children. He would do anything to save us from death, and he did it when he sent Jesus as the sacrifice to pay for our sins. The animal in the garden was the first blood sacrifice and Jesus was the last. It was the model God used to demonstrate the cost of sin and the devastating impact it has on our lives. But it is temporary.

In Psalms 90:10, Moses wrote, "Seventy years are given to us! Some even live to eighty. But even the best years are filled with pain and trouble; soon they disappear, and we fly away." Of course that's a generalization because some people live less and some live more, but none without pain and trouble. He added later, "Teach us to realize the brevity of life, so that we may grow in wisdom."

Just like God kept his word regarding death, he keeps it regarding life. Jesus tells us in John 3:16, "For this is how God loved the world: He gave his one and only Son, so that everyone who believes in him will not perish but have eternal life." We must not be angry with him when what he promised does indeed come to pass, because it applies to life in both realms. The end of the temporary need not be feared, and the promise of the eternal can be anticipated with hope.

Our deathbed prayers are not fruitless; whether or not they change the outcome for our loved ones, the prayers are evidence of the condition of our souls because there can be no pain of loss if there was never any joy of possession. Being filled with love is infinitely better than being devoid of this most heavenly of qualities. It helps us to understand the heart of God as he looked into the garden and saw his beloved leaving him, knowing that it would be a long wait until he could be with them again. And in this moment we become somewhat closer to him as we recognize that he completely understands our suffering. And that is good.

Anxiety: Part 1

Q: I have been having some anxiety, worry, and questions about a specific topic. Why, if it is so easy to find the Lord and get saved, does it say in Matthew that many will not enter

Heaven? If it is easy to get saved why wouldn't many enter into Heaven?

A: I would say it's a good thing that you have these questions because it shows that it matters to you. I would dispute one of your thoughts, though, about it being easy to get saved. I don't think it's easy to really get saved; I think, as many areas of Matthew point out, that people like the idea of getting saved but not the reality of it. The concept of easy comes from the fact that Jesus did all the work on the cross and we don't have to pay the price for our sins. But once someone confesses their sins and accepts Jesus as his or her Savior, they have to follow him— that's the first thing he told each of his disciples when he met them and called them into ministry: "Follow me." Following Jesus means not following your own way anymore, and this is the root of what Jesus talks about. I'll use Matthew 7:21 as the basis for answering your concerns: "Not everyone who calls out to me, 'Lord! Lord!' will enter the Kingdom of Heaven. Only those who actually do the will of my Father in heaven will enter."

What is the will of the Father? To love God and love your neighbor. Jesus said these were the two most important commandments. If you love God, you will love the people he loves, which is your neighbor (pretty much anybody you meet on this side of heaven, including unfriendly neighbors), and by doing so you won't do things like murder, steal, cheat, hate, lust after, and dishonor them, which covers the rest of the commandments.

So people who just "believe" in order to get out of going to hell probably aren't succeeding because saving your own skin is not the same as offering your life to God. And it's hard. Most people are lazy and don't want to do any work; not that "works" will save you, as some religions preach, but work such as loving God and loving your neighbor shows evidence that you want to be a true follower, doing what Jesus did while he was here.

A million other places in the Bible God says, "Don't be afraid." I want to repeat that to you: Don't be afraid. If you've placed your faith in Jesus you are saved from eternity in hell. You might not be saved from trouble here, though, because following Jesus is hard and some people won't like that you do it or even try to do it. But press on. You are his child and you will fail at times. He loves you and will help you by correcting and guiding you; you will grow and you will become closer to him as you "work out your salvation"—Paul uses those words in one of his letters and I love the visual that it gives of trying and falling and getting up again, and moving forward. If you have children you know what it's like to pick them up and give them a gentle push in the right direction. God is an outstanding and endlessly loving Father. You matter to him and he won't give up on you. The work for you now, as I see it expressed in the Scriptures, is to develop your relationship with him, to grow and flex your spiritual muscles as you follow Jesus. Don't be afraid.

Anxiety: Part 2

Q: Do you have any advice on dealing with a child with anxiety? I just don't think I want to put her on medicine.

A: I can tell you from my experience and observation that much of a child's personality and social development comes from what they see modeled in their parents during the most formative years. This is neither good nor bad, just a fact; you are a product of your upbringing, just like your husband, just like me, just like my wife. I've seen our kids take on good and bad characteristics that both of us have displayed.

I agree with your resistance to simply throwing them on some prescription drug. That seems to be the easy way out for many parents because it removes the need to deal with the real person inside and the real persons (us) who have directly influenced them.

My first thought is to understand anxiety. The dictionary describes it as fear or distress caused by danger or misfortune. That isn't always unhealthy as there are many reasons to have those feelings. It's how we respond to them that measures our health. I was reading over our last conversation and it seems like you might suffer from some of this, which would naturally be transferred to your child. This isn't a judgment, it's just an observation. So what do we do about it?

I would have an open and honest conversation with your child about your own fears and how you struggle with trusting

4

God. There is nothing wrong with being transparent to your children when it comes to helping them develop their own walk with God. Regardless of where she is in her knowledge of him, you have a knowledge of him, and it's better that she doesn't think that life is a walk in the park—it takes work, and her parents aren't perfect either; God gives us second and third (and seemingly countless) chances, just like you give her when you correct or discipline her because you still love her and want her to grow into a beautiful and strong young woman.

She feels and becomes what she sees and hears. Work on your modeling of Christian humility by being very open with her. Help her to be comfortable making mistakes and knowing that she is welcome to grow along with you, that you are both on the same path to being the wonderful creation God intends you to be, that he is patient with you and you will be patient with her.

I struggle with the idea of recommending personal counseling for her, although that is a good next step if your own work doesn't produce the results you think are appropriate. My struggle with the idea comes from experiences with counselors who often have their own baggage that hasn't been unpacked. I don't want to blow my own horn, but my points of view and my relationship with God have come from being uncomfortably vulnerable and aware of my own weaknesses. I truly believe that the only time God will really work with people is when they finally realize they need his help. That means visiting the scary place of admitting the need and being open to his changes.

Q: Oh my goodness. You are very correct in saying I am the same way. I think we have talked about anxiety in front of her because my husband is on medication for his and I have found ways to cope with mine like Bible reading, praying, or listening to music. I don't want her going down the medicine route. I have a lot of fears and anxieties and I am devastated that we could be the reason for our daughter being like this. Thank you so much for your absolute honesty, I would rather have that than you sugarcoat my ears with what I want to hear. I trust your judgment and advice. Thank you so much!

A: You are very welcome. Another thought is to ask her to share what her fears are if she is old enough to articulate them. Make sure she isn't afraid to be outspoken about them. If she's hearing discussions about finances, she might be afraid of running out of food or not having a roof over her head. If she hears other kids talking about abuse from their parents, maybe she's afraid of that happening to her. If she's afraid of the dark, it's a great time to teach about the Light that lives within and can never be extinguished and that he has conquered all that is evil.

Do not be above apologizing to her for your own fears, that you are still working on trust, that it's something everyone has to deal with for all of life; it's the reason you (and she) can always turn to God because he will never break your trust or fail you. Understanding that Christianity is a journey is better for her than thinking it's some type of mountaintop experience she should have and never come down from—that is damaging because it's not reality. This world is not our home. But God didn't send Jesus to take us out of the world; he sent him to help us walk while we are in it.

Drinking

Q: Is it okay for me to drink once in a while? My church doesn't think so and I am confused. I'm not an alcoholic.

A: "Don't be drunk with wine, because that will ruin your life. Instead, be filled with the Holy Spirit." (Ephesians 5:18)

Many religious organizations have policies that prohibit drinking alcohol, and they use this verse as their basis. But that misses the mark. Paul was using drunkenness as an example of the consequences of excess. He suggests instead, that if you're going to go overboard, then completely abandon yourself to the Holy Spirit.

The lesson here is to control yourself—in fact, self-control is one of the fruits of the Spirit listed in Galatians 5:22-23, which would mean it's included in the perks you get with salvation. As mature, reasoning, sensible believers, we should responsibly manage potential excesses of anything: food, work, play, sleep, money, debt. And, yes, alcohol.

But drinking, in and of itself, is not a sin. Many will point to the very first recorded miracle that Jesus did: he turned water into wine at the wedding celebration in Cana—and it wasn't grape juice as some detractors try to argue. Evidence of this is in the way the master of ceremonies questioned the groom: "A host always serves the best wine first. Then, when everyone has had a lot to drink, he brings out the less expensive wine. But you have kept the best wine until now." (John 2:10)

There is also Scripture that guides us in how we should conduct ourselves around people who have a new belief or those who are plagued with uncertainty. Paul gives good counsel when he talks about exercising our spiritual maturity with caution: "But you must be careful so that your freedom does not cause others with a weaker conscience to stumble." (1 Corinthians 8:9)

He goes on to warn against forcing our convictions on others who haven't yet arrived at the same conclusions, even going as far as highlighting with quote marks those with "superior knowledge" who are actually hurting new believers by shoe-horning them into patterns of action before they are ready or in agreement; "And when you sin against other believers by encouraging them to do something they believe is wrong, you are sinning against Christ."

So whether you drink alcohol or abstain, or whether you choose to exercise your many freedoms with abandon or restrain yourself, is your life glorifying to God or causing misery among the saints? On the fringes of this conversation are a couple of supplemental questions that need asked and the answers will likely be very personal: Whatever it is that you're consuming to excess, why is there a need for it? And: What kind of stimulant can satisfactorily replace a right relationship with God? Examine your priorities and you might surprise yourself.

Speaking in Tongues

Q: Do you speak in tongues? If so, or if not, what is your belief about them?

A: Hi! I don't have that gift, but here is what Paul writes: "Well, my brothers and sisters, let's summarize. When you meet together, one will sing, another will teach, another will tell some special revelation God has given, one will speak in tongues, and another will interpret what is said. But everything that is done must strengthen all of you. No more than two or three should speak in tongues. They must speak one at a time, and someone must interpret what they say. But if no one is present who can interpret, they must be silent in your church meeting and speak in tongues to God privately." (1 Corinthians 14:26-28)

This is from a passage in which Paul is talking about orderly worship. My personal experience has been that the people I've seen and heard speaking in tongues have no one interpreting and it is meaningless garble, usually done in company with others doing the same thing, so it's basically just mass confusion. It doesn't bring glory to God if people are confused or afraid. The people doing it become very defensive, almost hostile, when questioned. Read the whole chapter for Paul's complete dissertation on this because it really is very straightforward.

In many places the Bible mentions spiritual gifts; God grants them to us along with the presence of the Holy Spirit when we trust Jesus for salvation from our sins. It also says different people are given different gifts, but all to bring unity to the body of believers and glory to God. If anything we're doing fails in that work, then it is not of God, but of the devil. And the Bible very clearly states that no person and no gift is more important than another. I'm suspicious of any gifts that are only exposed on Saturday nights at 11:00 on a cable TV channel with sponsors and commercial breaks; God does not perform miracles based on tight production schedules or according to ratings charts. He certainly does not expect us to commercialize and monetize what he has given us for free. Spiritual gifts are also not the exclusive domain of highly-polished, seminary-trained, and contractually-obligated religious leaders—see Peter, the awkward former fisherman and three-time denier of Christ, who raises a girl from the dead in Acts 9:40.

Any time we find ourselves in a situation where a purported spiritual gift is being used in a questionable manner or presented as if it's available only to a select few or wielded as an attempt to bludgeon someone into submission, we need to run away, and fast. A very wise young missionary friend once told me, "If I am able to convince someone that they need Jesus, then someone else can convince them that they don't." We can share our gifts, but it's the Holy Spirit who convinces. And he does it in a voice that can be understood.

Is Jesus also God?

Q: Sir, I have a question. I don't know how to answer one of my friend's questions. My belief is the opposite of hers. The question is "Was Jesus Christ God or not?" I believe he is God even though I can't explain exactly why. Her religion believes he is not and that when he was crucified he was talking to someone; she keeps telling me Jesus was speaking to the real God. Can you please help me?

A: Don't feel too bad that you're struggling to explain something that you know inherently in your soul but can't find the right words; as humans we don't have the full capacity to understand spiritual matters. Faith means I believe what Jesus says even though I can't quite grasp all of it. Jesus was sent to earth as God in the flesh; it is God revealing himself to us in such a way that we can better know him. For generations God spoke to us through the prophets and he gave us the Ten Commandments, but finally he came in human form. Then when Jesus returned to heaven, he sent us the Holy Spirit to live directly inside us to help us with discernment. God is so concerned with restoring our relationship with him—the kind of personal relationship he had in the Garden of Eden when he walked and talked with his creation—that he used every option available to accomplish it. Heaven will be the place where we finally come together completely. Let me give you several verses that I believe clearly declare Jesus as God.

*****

"He existed in the beginning with God." (John 1:2)

"No one has ever seen God. But the unique One, who is himself God, is near to the Father's heart. He has revealed God to us." (John 1:18)

"The Father and I are one." (John 10:30)

"Don't you believe that I am in the Father and the Father is in me? The words I speak are not my own, but my Father who lives in me does his work through me." (John 14:10)

"For God was in Christ, reconciling the world to himself, no longer counting people's sins against them. And he gave us this wonderful message of reconciliation." (2 Corinthians 5:19)

"For in Christ lives all the fullness of God in a human body."
(Colossians 2:9)

*****

It's not easy to grasp because our sinful human minds are limited. That's why faith is so important; to believe something we can't see or totally understand. When Paul was wrapping up his first letter to Timothy, he wrote this: "At just the right time Christ will be revealed from heaven by the blessed and only almighty God, the King of all kings and Lord of all lords. He alone can never die, and he lives in light so brilliant that no human can approach him. No human eye has ever seen him, nor ever will. All honor and power to him forever!"

When it says, "[God] alone can never die" then we can realize why it became necessary for him to come to earth in the flesh, flesh that is holy and flawless and can represent the perfect sacrifice that was required to die in the place of our sin and imperfection. Reading verses like this, trying to imagine a light so brilliant that I can't approach, it makes me think of trying to view a solar eclipse; you can't see it with the naked eye as it can permanently damage your vision. But you can look at it through special lenses. Jesus is our special lens to see God—and he is the lens through which God can look at us!

Premarital Sex

Q: I'm really stuck and I need help. I'm in my early 20s and I have this desire to try out sex because I have never done it before! But I'm scared because I feel the moment I try it out I will not only upset the Father, also that my destiny will be ruined. What should I do?

A: The Holy Spirit is very strong in you to feel that kind of apprehension. It's a good thing. According to Scripture, sex is reserved for marriage. Genesis 2:24 says, "This explains why a man leaves his father and mother and is joined to his wife, and the two are united into one." Some translations use the term "one flesh." This is the union that bonds a man and woman together unlike any other connection that is possible in this world, and it is reflective of the intimacy of the Father, Son, and Spirit, as they are one in unity and relationship.

Violating God's perfect design for man and woman will upset him. And it will change the way you think and live and the direction of your future. This certainly doesn't mean that God can't forgive or won't heal, but scars will always remain. The solution is to get married. That sounds simplistic, but it really is easier than it sounds if you can find a woman who also wants to honor God with her body and is willing to wait for a man who wants to follow God with his life. It is worth the wait.

Paul writes in Ephesians 5:21, "Submit to one another out of reverence for Christ." The number of young single people is growing. The clock keeps ticking and from conversations I've had it seems like many of them are waiting for the perfect mate. Newsflash: Prince Charming and Sleeping Beauty are fictitious characters. Don't expect perfection. Find a boy or girl who appeals to you and with whom you have some common interests. Determine that he or she is a dedicated follower of Christ. Get married. God will help you make it work.

Difficulties are inevitable. But the longer one waits, the higher the likelihood of hormones overtaking good intentions. Experimenting or checking to see if everything fits right does not bring glory to God. Added trouble due to promiscuity—and memories of multiple indiscretions and broken promises—will only make the marriage journey harder.

I counseled one young couple that there will be times when they wake up and wonder how they could have ever made a commitment to that wretch lying on the other side of the bed. And sleeping on the couch out of anger or hurt is also a possibility regardless of how dreamy life seems today. Go into the relationship with your eyes wide open and with the clear understanding that sometimes the only way we can love our spouses is to remember that Jesus loves them. And that's enough.

I will say from 35 years of my own marriage that there is no such thing as "being ready" to get married. No one has any idea what life will look like after you say, "I do." The person you think you know is a product of a whole life that existed before you ever entered the picture. This is another reason I believe in young marriages; less interference from outside influences that can complicate the union. Growing through life and experiences together is better than coming at them from sharply different viewpoints and entrenched positions.

But the sex issue: having relations with women other than the one to whom you will dedicate the rest of your life is never a good thing. You do not forget, and neither will she.

Q: So what if there are chances of settling down with her?

A: Settling down?

Q: Like marry her!

A: Yes! Marry her. Too many people in modern times think that living together is the same thing. It's not even close. Making a vow of marriage, pledging "Till death do us part," is the kind of commitment God designed. It is the way he loves us, with an endless love, through all of our doubts and dalliances, with constant forgiveness and a willingness always to restore the relationship no matter what the offense. This is what makes a truly great man and a truly great marriage. Jesus said in Matthew 19:6, "Since they are no longer two but one, let no one split apart what God has joined together."

I questioned your question because you said "chances" of settling down. An engagement or a serious commitment is not a license for sex; a marriage certificate and a ring and a public ceremony before God and witnesses is a good place to start, and if there are good friends who can help to hold you accountable that's even better.

Being godly is not easy. It's why he gave us his Holy Spirit to help. But following his perfect plan yields peace and joy—and a satisfaction unlike you ever knew existed. His command to believers is that we not be "unequally yoked," which means partnered to those who are not followers of Jesus. That's hard, too, because there are scores of appealing women out there. Keep your eyes on him and he will lead you to the right one.

Q: OK, thank you very much. I will try to maintain.

My parents are against my marriage

Q: I'm having a challenge in my relationship. My folks are against me getting married to my fiancé, but I trust God and his promises. What should I do?

A: Have you had an honest, open conversation with your parents? Have you included your fiancé in that conversation? If you choose to get married, it's for life and all of you will spend a lot of time together. It is extremely valuable to have everyone in agreement if at all possible. The Bible says to honor your parents. That doesn't mean to go against what God is saying to you, but you need to respect their thinking and listen; they may have valid concerns.

It also says that the two of you will become one, which means you will cling to her like life itself and honor her over your parents if it comes to differences that can't be resolved. Will you be able to do that? Are you aware of the seriousness of the marriage union? It makes you one, never to be divided, and your life will be dedicated to her.

I highly recommend all of you sitting down together and praying for wisdom and guidance before addressing your own concerns. Seek to honor God first. Have civilized discourse. Be sensitive to the hearts and minds of everyone. These are tender and important times and will set the path for years to come. It's better to deal now with this trouble than later. It may be a time of growth and healing for the whole family.

Q: My parents are not supporting me, but in the beginning they did. I have prayed over it and I keep seeing her in my dreams. They disapprove of my marriage because of old traditions. Which I know means nothing. Hope you will put me and my marital issues in your prayers.

A: I certainly don't know the whole story of what is going on. Traditions are good and they can help you stay rooted to culture and family, but Jesus was always in heated conversations with the religious leaders of his day over their substituting traditions in place of God's laws. The very basics of marriage is that a man and woman come together in a one-flesh relationship and remain committed to each other for life. "Let not man separate what God has joined together." Both participants must be willing to submit to each other for the good of the union, honoring God in body, mind, and spirit, and staying firmly planted in his Word so they continue getting the direction they need for managing life and family. I can't imagine any parents denying that holy purpose in your lives. Honor God above all.

Dear God, please bless my brother as he looks for peace and direction. Give him wisdom beyond his age and experience. Bless his parents. Bless his fiancé as she watches him strive to follow you. Make him a man who is Christlike in every way. In the name of Jesus, Amen.

The Fear of the Lord

Q: What does it mean to fear the Lord?

A: Psalms 2:11 says, "Serve the Lord with reverent fear." That's not God. It's a verse that pops up in devotionals and on bumper stickers and sometimes you'll see it on a billboard or a sign in a front yard. But it is an incomplete verse and it represents an incomplete God. And I believe it is the reason why so many people have no interest in him—and why those with even a fledgling interest don't grow closer. Who wants to live in fear?

The rest of the verse says, "and rejoice with trembling." Let me paint a different picture of God for you to consider. He is a God who yearns for intimacy with us and he moves heaven and earth, literally, to resolve anything that would threaten that relationship, hence the ongoing battle to save people from sin and death.

In the military we were required to serve temporary duty assignments; they were missions classified as "unaccompanied" which means we couldn't take family. One year I spent three months freezing in a Montana winter before I could see my wife.

When we finally met again I remember trembling in joy. I wanted to crush her to me, but also I wanted to hold her at arms-length and just look at her and talk and catch up on all the missed time. But I didn't want to say or do anything that might disrespect her or break the moment or negatively affect our reunion. That was reverent fear.

We completely miss God when we think of him as an ogre or a fearsome judge holding a hammer ready to smash us. We can respect the fact that he will judge those who reject Jesus; fear is reserved for those who hate God and have earned their destruction. But that's the last thing he wants to do; he doesn't want us to be afraid, but to love him so he can love us— intimately, not just through a page in a dusty book.

All over the Bible you will see him say to the people who encounter him, "Don't be afraid." When you think fear and trembling, think quivering in anticipation, desperate for a connection with the one who knows you better than you know yourself, one whose true rage is focused on anything that will take you away from him. That's God.

The Coming of the Holy Spirit

Q: Good day to you. I love reading your testimonials about Jesus Christ. I want to know how did you know you received the Holy Ghost? Please, this is something I have a real struggle with.

A: Hi! In John 16 Jesus talks about the coming of the Holy Spirit, that when he comes he will bring conviction of sin, of righteousness, and of judgment. There is a lot of teaching in the world about the things you have to do to get the Holy Spirit but it's something that Jesus does, not man. He said he had to return to heaven or else he couldn't send him to us. Peter said we have to believe in Jesus, then the Spirit would come, which goes along with what Jesus said. I don't think many people have these big mountaintop experiences and flashes of lightning when they're "filled with the Spirit" or "Holy Ghost fire." You may hear teaching about the baptism of the Holy Spirit and some will preach on the days of Pentecost in the New Testament when thousands were converted and started speaking other languages. That sounds romantic and exciting, but they were special events at special times that God used to advance the message of the Gospel into the world.

I think sometimes people expect to finally "arrive" and everything will start to make sense and the world will turn smoothly. But it doesn't usually look like we think it should look. Living the Christian life is hard. It requires lots and lots of days of seeing only pain and misery because that's what the world is filled with. Following Jesus requires sacrifice; that's what he came to do and he said, "Follow me." Read this from Peter: "Dear friends, don't be surprised at the fiery trials you are going through, as if something strange were happening to you. Instead, be very glad—for these trials make you partners with Christ in his suffering, so that you will have the wonderful joy of seeing his glory when it is revealed to all the world." (1 Peter 4:12-13)

Praying is sometimes just a matter of grinding along, and we won't always hear the voice of God as a typical or expected reply to our concerns and requests; Jesus prayed in the Garden for a way out of going to the cross and he didn't get any answer except silence. Regardless, we must live according to the word and will of God, and that means loving him and loving your fellow man. Neither are easy, but it's your perseverance that marks your faithfulness. Intimacy with Jesus means doing what he did. You won't likely get your glory here, but only when you get to heaven.

But everyone who believes gets the Holy Spirit; he fills you when you confess that you're a sinner and trust Jesus for salvation. He "shows up" or becomes evident in your life when you start obeying his promptings. It's like the old saying, "When the student is ready the teacher will appear." He's already in us but waiting on us. Obedience is the catalyst to a more robust relationship with the Spirit as he draws us closer to God. Obedience equals blessings, which makes us desire even more intimacy and joy.

The novelty of salvation—leaving a path of sure death and destruction and moving into a whole and personal relationship with God—shouldn't wear off, but looking for something that he didn't promise will leave you discouraged and disillusioned. It all comes down to humble obedience, which sounds boring and mundane but it's the proof of your belief. And God blesses us more as we obey him more. Jesus isn't lost to history in the pages of your New Testament, nor is he out of reach in heaven; he still speaks to us today through the Holy Spirit. Jesus called him the "Advocate" and in preparing his disciples for his coming Jesus said, "He will bring me glory by telling you whatever he receives from me." He's still talking and he's still leading. Follow him today, just one step at a time, and you will see amazing things happen.

Self-esteem and Career Paths

Q: Hello, how are you? I am asking for special prayer. I have some unstable emotions as well as self-esteem issues and I'm at a crossroad for choosing a career path. Thank you, I look forward to hearing from you. God bless you.

A: Hi. I'm great! Hey, I want to remind you of who you are. In Jeremiah 1:5, God tells the writer that "I knew you before I formed you in your mother's womb." That means God knows you, too, and he has plans for you that existed long before you were ever conceived. Whatever your mom or dad has done or not done, or planned, or made mistakes about—or anything—is second place to what God has in mind for you. You were created; you were designed to fit into this time and place and to have a relationship with God, first, and then everything else. You are special to him and he loves you. He loves you so much that he sent Jesus to pay for your sins to ensure that you would have a chance to be saved from them and still be reunited with him in spirit here on earth, but reunited completely in body and spirit for eternity in heaven.

As far as a career path: I would suggest that you don't get too overly concerned with the end of the picture before you even get started. If you get so focused on the "perfect job" you might actually miss it because you pass up opportunities that could set you on the path to it. What I mean is, take almost any job versus sitting on the sidelines waiting for your dream job. Get out there and work because you will be around people, and people know other people, and they will see your skills and abilities and then things kind of just happen. And while you're working, work "as unto the Lord" (Colossians 3:23) because you will be reflecting him to all those around you. But only if you are out there. Make a plan, but be willing to go wherever events take you. Why?

Because you can trust in God. He knows how he built you, he knows your skills and talents, and he also knows the future. He will make good come out of what you think might not be so great.

You can trust in his knowledge of how he made you, but he also gave you the free will to choose to move forward or sit on your hands. Don't sit. And rejoice in the fact that he is watching over you and will shape your path. I love you brother.

Dear God, please bless my young brother with the peace that comes with your presence. Give him the power that comes with your Spirit living in him. Give him awareness of your direction. Give him the strength to follow you. In Jesus' name, Amen.

Jesus on Race, Economics, and Class

Q: In Matthew 15:21-28 there's a drama with a Canaanite woman, the disciples, and Jesus. The lady pleads for her daughter's healing, the disciples want to chase her away, and Jesus tells the lady that he came only for the lost sheep of Israel. Jesus sounded sarcastic but the lady's wish was granted; her daughter was healed at once! Great faith! What's the meaning of this passage? Please help.

A: Yes, it includes a lot of underlying friction that isn't addressed very frequently in the church: race relations, economic divisions, class distinctions.

The text says she was a Gentile woman, two strikes against her in that day and age. Women didn't generally address men, and the Jews and Gentiles had nothing to do with each other. So Jesus was testing her faith. He tried it first by ignoring her. Second, he allowed his disciples to attempt to dismiss her. Third, he distinguished himself as a preacher to the Jews only, the children of Israel. Fourth, and finally, he proposed that she wasn't good enough for his message (comparing her to a dog eating the children's food).

Nothing dissuaded her. She had entered the conversation by addressing him as "Lord, Son of David," indicating that she realized he was a Jew, since David was the historic king of the

Jews, and giving him the honor of calling him Lord, which transcended race and culture and location. Jesus marveled at her faith, for so many of his own people didn't recognize these things. And since Jesus is God, he knew what was coming, what she would ask, and whether she could be effectively turned away. So he used the situation as a learning moment for his disciples and now, since it's recorded for us, a lesson thousands of years later.

The lesson is that if you believe in Jesus as Lord, never give up on your requests for his help and work in your life and the lives of those for whom you may intercede. He is Lord of all, there is no line that divides any of us from him or prevents anyone from approaching him. His delay in answering may simply be a test of your faith and to see if you really want what you're asking. You asked a good question because it's an amazing story. Thanks, because it made me dig into it!

Tattoos

Q: Can you please send me the verse that says not to have tattoos on our bodies? I want to show it to my husband because he says he doesn't believe it . . . and I truly don't want him to get one . . . thanks.

A: "Do not cut your bodies for the dead, and do not mark your skin with tattoos. I am the Lord." (Leviticus 19:28)

This verse is from a section in my Bible titled Holiness in Personal Conduct. You would think it was written in a foreign language considering the widespread lack of adherence to the general principles contained within. Lots of Christians claim "freedom from the law" since Jesus came, but he himself said he didn't come to abolish the law but to fulfill it. So people pick and choose what they want to believe.

I say all that to say this: Why does a person get a tattoo? Some get a deceased loved one's epitaph—and we mutilate the living to honor the dead; yet Jesus died and was raised to bring new life and that's where our focus should remain. Some honor a sports team or any number of other things; honor them above

God? Some use them for decoration; as if God didn't create us in his own beautiful image?

*****

In the time since this question was originally asked I've done some additional research in the public domain. According to several polls, nearly a third of the population has at least one tattoo, and that's not specific to one section of the world more than another; it's globally representative. And the reasons stated weigh heavily in favor of two responses: "It makes me feel rebellious" and "It makes me feel sexy." So again I ask the question I first asked: Why does a person get a tattoo? That answer obviously is very personal but it will tell you a lot about yourself and what you believe.

And what do you do if you're feeling convicted about this? Well, what do you do about anything that convicts you? Bring it to God and confess it. Forgiveness is more permanent than ink.

Help! My wife caught me cheating

Q: Please pray for me and my wife to reconcile. We are on the brink of divorcing after I was cheating on her and she discovered it. I am embarrassed with my actions. I apologized but was not forgiven. My wife has packed her bags and will be leaving on Saturday. Please help.

A: The first step is to confess your sin to God. You've sinned against him because he is the creator of marriage and the one-flesh union that seals it. He will forgive a contrite heart and restore your relationship with him. And you must get serious about your relationship with him and your wife. No one else can come between it. No one. Your attempts to reconcile with your wife are going to need her acceptance and the belief that you are sincere; I would suggest that you have a long journey. Let me share something I wrote a while ago regarding a counseling session I had with a couple in a similar situation:

*****

"So guard your heart; remain loyal to the wife of your youth." (Malachi 2:15b)

A couple came to me for counseling. They were having problems in their marriage. They sat on the other side of the desk with arms crossed and scowls on their faces; only inches separated them but they were miles apart. Things were bad enough that her bags were packed at home and she was planning to leave after this appointment. No pressure. "Lord help me," I silently prayed.

I asked them to remember back to when they first dated. They couldn't wait to see each other after work and on the weekends. He would buy her special little gifts to make her smile. She would smile. She would take hours in the bathroom to make sure she looked her best when he came over. He would wait. And it was always worth it.

Then I pointed at each of them and reminded them that those two kids were still in there; the fire that once roared may have shrunken to a tiny ember barely smoldering under the ashes of time and turmoil, but it's still there. Take the time to find it, blow on it, coax it into a burning flame.

Our marriages are precious. They are ordained by God to bring glory to him and joy to us. They make us complete. Don't let the enemies of resentment or forgetfulness destroy yours. Don't hold onto pains that are past. Forgive. Look deep into the eyes of your mate and rediscover that girl or boy who once attracted your fascination and melted your heart. It takes work, but they're still in there.

She unpacked her bags.

*****

You both have a lot of work to do. Your wife is welcome to communicate with me if she is willing. It honors God to forgive and reconcile relationships, just as he has done with all of mankind who has cheated against him by loving other gods. But know that she is very hurt. You will probably have to start all over again with her to regain her trust—the courting process, dating, making her the center of your life (after God). If she leaves, it does not stop your obligation to love her in whatever way you can. She may need time to think and reflect and for the

21

Lord to work on her heart; seeing you may initially only cause pain, so give her space.

Dear God, please bless this couple. Their marriage is ordained by you and can only be sustained by you. I pray that your power will be manifest as you draw both of them to yourself. Heal where there is pain, fill them with peace where there is turmoil. Lord, I know you can do anything and all things in the name of Jesus, so that's how I will ask. Amen.

The Company You Keep

Several years of correspondence from different areas of the world have resulted in some very similar conversations in which the same topic keeps coming up. The kind of people with whom we associate definitely has an impact on our own social and spiritual development, and the effectiveness of our witness. The following section includes some of the replies to those questions.

*****

"Bad company corrupts good character." (1Corinthians 15:33)

Don't be surprised when you track mud all through the house if you just spent the whole day walking in it. Too many Christians think then can socialize almost exclusively with unbelievers and not have it affect their own conduct. It doesn't work that way.

What you hear and what you see on a regular basis will begin to shape your identity. Are your friends encouraging you to do what is right in God's eyes, or in their own? You can usually tell by how well things are going for you. Or not.

Changing your life can be as simple as changing your friends. Real friends care more about your spiritual health than whether or not you like what they say; truth isn't something to fear but to embrace. So if all you ever hear is what you want to hear, it's time to question their authenticity. Sometimes you need a push, not a pat on the head.

*****

...ds like something Paul wrote about being unequally yoked together with unbelievers, that light and darkness don't mix. Catch it now before God has to put you through the heavy stain cycle.

*****

"I meant that you are not to associate with anyone who claims to be a believer yet indulges in sexual sin, or is greedy, or worships idols, or is abusive, or is a drunkard, or cheats people. Don't even eat with such people." (1 Corinthians 5:11)

When I talk about guarding yourself from bad people, about being aware of the company you keep and how it affects your spiritual growth, some of the responses I get indicate that maybe I haven't been clear.

If we were supposed to stay completely away from the wicked, Jesus never would have come. His model of sharing the Gospel put him squarely in the middle of the lost and the evil; he brought light where there was only darkness and hope where there was none.

Paul clarified this in his letter better than me—he states without any room for confusion that we are not to associate with believers who choose to go on sinning. They should be avoided at all costs and, even more harshly in other passages, they should be unwelcome in the fellowship of believers—they should be ejected from our church services; they are like a poison that spreads.

Save your ministry efforts for unbelievers, he writes, because they are everywhere and "You would have to leave this world to avoid people like that." But don't play games with Christians who refuse to take their Lord seriously; in this case acceptance equals agreement.

*****

"Peter answered, 'You are the Messiah, the Son of the living God.'" (Matthew 16:18)

"Peter denied it, this time with an oath. 'I don't even know the man.'" (Matthew 26:72)

In just a few short chapters we see Peter going from bold declarer to furtive denier. It can happen to anyone.

A friend of mine came back from a men's conference and volunteered to speak in front of the church about the awesome presence of God and how it had changed his life. Before long he had left his wife and run off with another woman. No amount of counsel could deter him.

Beware of the company you keep and the strategies of the enemy. I have no doubt that Peter and my friend had authentic experiences with God. But their own fears—and their own weaknesses—overcame them when the pressure was on.

Stay close to God. Be honest enough with yourself to admit that you are susceptible to attack; avoid places where you know you are at risk. This walk we have as believers is no Sunday afternoon stroll, it is a dangerous trip through a minefield. Hold tightly to the hand of the One who can lead you safely through it.

Tragedy

Q: I just came across something you wrote about God's love for us. Please help me understand this because I'm going through a crisis. My boyfriend died in a road accident two months ago, he was a believer too. Before starting off on that very fateful day, we spoke and I prayed for his journey, only to be told hours later that he was gone. Honestly, ever since he passed I can't bring myself to pray or read the Word; I feel like God has forsaken me.

A: I am so sorry to hear of your loss. It's okay to be upset. The effects of sin in the world include death among all of its horrors. When Jesus saw all the people mourning around the tomb of Lazarus, the passage says he was angry in his spirit—it even more highly emphasizes the need for his coming to save us from sin and everything it does to us.

Times like this it's hard to believe that God is good. But he is. And he's doing something in your life. You can use this to draw closer to him. He knows what it feels like to lose a loved one. That's one of the reasons we see the story of him losing Jesus to such a gruesome and violent death. You now know loss like not many others do. Marvel at the softness of your spirit. Be amazed at how much you can care. It's the heart of God in you: you were created in his image. Along with his joy you can feel his pain.

Do not stay in a place of sorrow. Look at the sunlight and the flowers. The verse that says he makes the rain to fall on the just and the unjust means that we all live with all of the conditions that happen in this world. Find a little piece of happiness in this dark time. Rejoice that you will see your boyfriend again. These days are temporary, eternity is forever. God is doing something good. He always is.

The Unsettled Mind

Q: I wonder if you could help me with something that has been on my mind for a few days now. I think I have a problem within myself with all the confusion I've been struggling with. Out of nowhere, questions pop up inside my head and I don't know where they came from. Though my mind is blank, they just come and mostly they give me anxiety and confusion. What do I do with this?

A: I guess it depends on what questions are popping up. In 1 Corinthians 14:33 Paul writes, "God is not a God of disorder but of peace." If you are having questions that are confusing or unsettling, they are not coming from God. If you are a Christian —meaning you have given your life to Christ and the Holy Spirit is living in you—then the thoughts aren't coming from Satan because God isn't going to share his space in you with the enemy. That leaves one option: your own flesh desires. We still have to fight against our old nature even though God has won our souls.

Paul also writes in Colossians 3:5: "So put to death the sinful, earthly things lurking within you. Have nothing to do with sexual immorality, impurity, lust, and evil desires." This was written to Christians and the counsel is not aimed only at sexual issues but anything that draws you away from holiness, and that list can be endless.

I will take exception to the first thing I said in that we can often feel confusion about holiness if we are resisting it. If God, through his Holy Spirit, is trying to prompt you to do good things, or things that you don't really want to do because of harmful and deeply established patterns of the past, it may be confusing because you are struggling against him. The solution to that kind of fight is to just surrender. Give in to the power of the Holy Spirit because he is significantly stronger than you and he won't give up. When you asked Jesus to be Lord of your life, you may sometimes have second thoughts but he doesn't. He is going to work tirelessly to shape you into the original creation he designed you to be from the beginning.

Q: In the past days and weeks, I've seen myself falling into the lust of my flesh and being immersed in the things of this world like watching certain things on TV. I feel convicted every time, and I've been wanting to stop but there are these days when I fail so hard and become desperate to stop for the Lord. I can always feel his presence but I still fail to turn my back to my fleshly desires, even if I wanted to so bad, I just fail. Now I learn that the Holy Spirit is the only one who will help me overcome, but I can't fully define what surrendering and repentance are and how to do them. I hope God will use you to help me with this.

A: In John 16:8 Jesus said he was sending the Holy Spirit and when he came he would convict the world of its sin, God's righteousness, and the coming judgment. But he never said he would force any of it on us. Obedience is a matter of your own personal will being surrendered. You have to decide to act according to the convictions he is placing in you. It's the reason there is sin in the world in the first place: Adam and Eve failed to obey what they knew was right. In your case, if it's something you're watching, cancel the channel or the entire service if that's what it takes to remove the temptation. If that decision isn't one you are allowed to make, then refuse to watch any television. It's like the alcoholic who decides to avoid not only bars but even restaurants that serve drinks. You have control over your choices and your spiritual maturity is on trial every time you have to make a decision. Obedience is the key. God will always forgive if you ask, but personally I get tired of going to him with my head hanging. So I guess my charge to you is to try harder; you have the power in you.

Dear God, please bless my brother with the ability to see the temptation coming before it's too close and the strength to resist it. In the name of Jesus, Amen.

Homosexuality

Q: I want to have a same sex relationship. I'm a gay but I'm also looking at what God promises. Sometimes I can't avoid myself and fall into lust. I hope you can give some quick advice that will help me.

A: Lots of churches want to pick out certain sins as worse than others. But all sin is hated by God. The Bible says homosexuality is sin. So you need to resist it, the same way you resist stealing or lusting or using God's name in vain.

Q: Thanks. My friend was asking me how do we avoid this kind of personality, since when we grew up we knew we were gay? Is there any way to live like what God desires for man?

A: Everyone is born as a sinner and that is the reason we sin; sin takes on countless forms. But Jesus came to save us from our sin, not so we would keep living in it. He said, "If any of you wants to be my follower, you must give up your own way, take up your cross daily, and follow me. If you try to hang on to your life, you will lose it. But if you give up your life for my sake, you will save it." (Luke 9:23-24)

So the question is, do you want to follow Jesus or do you want to follow your own desires? One way leads to heaven and the other to hell. Is homosexuality, or any other sin, worth losing your soul? "Taking up your cross" means learning how to carry a burden and still follow him. Jesus had to carry a literal cross and die for us. He decided to live in such a way that he honored God. If you want to honor God you must deny sin.

Your burden may be a desire for another man. You must learn to resist it. In the book of James it says, "So humble yourselves before God. Resist the devil, and he will flee from you." (James 4:7)

With the power of God you can defeat the desire to sin since the Holy Spirit lives in every believer. Are you a believer?

Q: Yes, I'm still a believer, even though I decided to leave my ministry as a Christian. Sometimes I ask him if he still loves me, and to guide me due to my situation in life. I trust him and love him but I'm not always blessed . . . honestly sometimes I lose my faith. And I ask if God is still alive? And if grant or answer my prayers. But then I'm than~ people who appreciate me and will give their time ~ story. So thank you.

A: God is very much alive and well. You must determine to follow him. Dabbling in sin makes your decision less credible. God isn't going to bless you if you are disobedient. Check your priorities and get them straight. If you don't take God seriously there's not much reason for him to take you seriously.

*****

I am convinced that pride is often what makes the Christian community ineffective. We choose to condemn homosexuality but we quickly look the other way when it comes to our own sins —we rate sins on a scale of which ones we are not committing at the time. But Jesus told us to love our neighbors as ourselves; there were no exceptions. Is that a hard concept? It probably is, based on the level of conflict that exists over this topic. The fact that a gay person might not live next door to you, or even anywhere in your neighborhood, and you don't have to make a conscious effort to relate to them, is no excuse for an unloving spirit toward people who are suffering from this particular sin— or from any sin; the sins that are popular are always going in and out of style.

There is a current push to make homosexuality normal and mainstream, regardless of what God says. It's a wasted effort, because public opinion will never change the rules of holiness. Nor does it change our responsibility to love our neighbors. But loving sinners does not mean approving of sin; God does not approve of sin, yet he loves us. And loving someone doesn't guarantee that your love will be received; a person who is bent on sinning will not immediately accept your love—maybe never —but you must continue to offer it. Even if it is received it may not be returned. Love anyway.

No change will ever take place if hate is all that sinners see from those who claim to follow a God of love and forgiveness. Pray about how you can live an authentic life, one that will be attractive to those who are searching but don't even know it. Be open to having a conversation with someone who doesn't think

you. Trust God to give you the words you will need. Instead
finding fault, use your energy finding ways to be Christlike.

Sexual Identity & Sexual Intercourse

Some additional commentary on human sexuality that was generated by the previous discussion:

"So God created human beings in his own image. In the image of God he created them; male and female he created them." (Genesis 1:27)

I was present at the births of both of our children. We had one girl and one boy, and there was no difficulty deciding which was which; it was quite obvious. The complications society is experiencing today with identity disorders has nothing to do with gender confusion and everything to do with spiritual confusion.

Lots of Christians seem to have trouble finding compassion for the LGBT community; if that sounds like you, please try harder. No matter how many letters are added to the category, God still loves them. But also, no matter how many parades or protests are held, he will not approve of sin—any type of sin.

Imagine a life of refusing to yield to a higher power, or demanding that the bar of acceptance be constantly lowered. It must be exhausting. But it is no different from any of us thinking that God should overlook our own sins, and tired, unrepentant heterosexuals are admitted to hell just as quickly as anyone else.

God is holy. He loves all of mankind equally. And he also judges equally; he doesn't discriminate—all sin qualifies to separate his created human beings from him. It's why he makes forgiveness available to any who will receive it. His acceptance and approval is based solely on belief in the life, death, and resurrection of Jesus. That is where true identity is found.

*****

"God abandoned them to do whatever shameful things their hearts desired. As a result, they did vile and degrading things with each other's bodies." (Romans 1:24)

Homosexuality is only half love; so is base heterosexuality. Sexual relations without the spiritual component is artificial, it's incomplete. God's abandonment was a result of men and women choosing to worship themselves instead of their Creator. Which prompts me to say this: sex isn't bad; bad sex is bad.

Sexual intercourse was designed to be the culmination of a total and permanent spiritual commitment between a man and a woman—the relationship originally known as marriage. The casual and temporary physical unions that we see all around us today do not qualify, and it is impossible to enjoy the freedom and exhilaration of an ordained relationship no matter how many ways you twist it.

The illusion that absolute sexual gratification can be experienced outside of a godly marriage is what has caused all of the existing variations; the number of perversions continues to grow and the perpetrators still aren't satisfied—and for good reason: God does not bless sin.

I don't wish to be overly graphic, but physical orgasm is not the ultimate climax, nor can it be achieved by redefining love into something other than what it was created to be: true climax is reached in the state of knowing that the man and woman who are joined together are not only partners in the flesh, but also in heart and mind, submitted to each other and to God and committed to fidelity—and forgiveness—for life; they are inseparable and have truly become one. It is the model presented to us by the Father, Son, and Spirit. There is nothing superior to it in this world or the next.

God's Original Name

Q: Based on ancient scriptures, what was/is the original name of our God, the Creator? Some books indicate Yahweh/ YHWH, Jehovah, Lord God. I have here a copy of the writing of the Name of God in Hebrew, but I don't know how to read it.

A: The historical name of God traced back to Hebrew manuscripts is best translated into English as YHWH. This spelling uses only consonant letters and removes vowels in order to make it impossible to pronounce or utter out loud. This was a direct response to the legitimate need to treat God with reverence and awe, but quickly turned into a sense of fear. It became—and still is in many areas of the world—forbidden to say the name, and if written it could never be altered or erased.

A significant problem exists with this view of God. There are dozens and dozens of verses in the Old and New Testaments where God tells us, either in his own words or through a message from a prophet or an angel, to not be afraid. If we look at God as revealed in all of Scripture, he is our heavenly Father, the one who brought us into the world and the one who desires to have a beautiful parent/child relationship with us. He repeatedly calls us to himself; he illustrates his love for us as a shepherd caring for his sheep, and as a hen gathering her chicks under a protective wing. Ultimately he sacrifices the life of his own Son to save us. That isn't a God to be feared, but a God to be adored.

Fear creates distance. God doesn't want us to be afraid of him; he wants to hold us, like the father in the parable of the prodigal son, who raced out to meet his lost son with open arms, to gather him and celebrate his return. Fear is man-made and destroys relationships. God is the opposite of that, longing for intimacy and friendship, and he showed it when he came to earth as a man and sat along the seashore eating and talking with his disciples.

Jesus spoke to this pattern of worship based on fear and he condemned it. The religious leaders of his day had made the relationship into a ritual, an impossible list of rules and regulations that perpetuated fear. He said, "You search the Scriptures because you think they give you eternal life. But the Scriptures point to me! Yet you refuse to come to me to receive this life." (John 5:39-40)

What you call him is less important than how you love him. We fail miserably when we revere the name as more important than the one who bears the name.

Remarriage

Q: Can I get married again?

A: I need to give this a more thorough answer than time permits.

I hesitated to give this question a quick reply because it came up during a discussion of difficult marriages and the consequences of unmet expectations, unpleasant discoveries, and unfaithfulness. It also happens to be one of the most contentious topics in the church and the most abused. I guess that should be expected since marriage is one of the closest issues to God's heart, which also explains the reason the enemy attacks it so relentlessly. But bad teaching leads to bad living, so understanding the truth is vital to our success. This is a lengthy answer so first we need a good foundation; let's see what Jesus says.

"But 'God made them male and female' from the beginning of creation. 'This explains why a man leaves his father and mother and is joined to his wife, and the two are united into one.'" (Mark 10:6-8a)

Godly marriage is designed to exist between one man and one woman, one time, for life. A married couple's unity models the unity of the Father, Son, and Holy Spirit.

"Since they are no longer two but one, let no one split apart what God has joined together." (Mark 10:8b-9)

Separation and divorce are man-made constructions bent on destroying what God has created and blessed. Every effort must be made to reconcile difficulties, up to and including sacrificing one's own will and desires for the good of the other, just like Jesus did on the cross for the salvation of mankind.

"Whoever divorces his wife and marries someone else commits adultery against her. And if a woman divorces her husband and marries someone else, she commits adultery." (Mark 10:11-12)

The marriage union is sacred. Any deviation from God's original plan dishonors God and causes more sin, violating his perfect design for humanity.

*****

It's likely that you will run into people who have decided to take advantage of what some have called the Exception Clause; it's how wedding ceremonies are justified for couples who have been previously married but are now divorced. Let's look at it: Jesus answered this question very clearly, but his words have been twisted today just like they were twisted then.

"And I say to you, whoever divorces his wife, except for sexual immorality, and marries another, commits adultery; and whoever marries her who is divorced commits adultery." (Matthew 19:9)

The Pharisees were trying to trap Jesus into approving their methods, including divorce for any and every reason. He had already debunked their first argument by explaining that Moses had only permitted divorce as a concession to the hardness of their hearts; they were brutal and vicious to their suddenly and conveniently unappealing wives, and issuing a certificate of divorce was a better option than abandonment or violence. This was no model to follow and it was a shameful solution to the ungodly treatment of their women, and Jesus made that point.

But here we address the Exception. The exception Jesus granted for divorce is sexual immorality, or fornication; it was for the discovery that one of the participants had been involved in sexual relations prior to the upcoming formal union. This is the reason Joseph planned to break his engagement with Mary. She was pregnant but they hadn't yet consummated their union sexually, so the situation seemed obvious—the passage records that Joseph was a righteous man; in marrying her he would have been committing adultery because she appeared to have already had sexual relations, "united into one" with another man, effectively making her a married woman.

Note: The sexual union, the "one flesh" relationship that uniquely joins a man and woman, is what marries them to each other, not a wedding ring or piece of paper. For many readers the realization of this truth may bring a lot of tears and the need for confession and healing. But that's what God does: he forgives and heals.

Joseph's mind was quickly changed when the angel of the Lord appeared to him and revealed that the child in Mary's womb had been conceived by the Holy Spirit. So she was innocent of any offense; Mary was not guilty of a previous encounter that would have united her to another man, and Joseph wouldn't be committing adultery by marrying her. He followed the orders of the Lord and took her as his wife.

The majority of today's religious organizations make exceptions of all kinds, just like the religious leaders in Jesus' day. Adultery, which by definition is sexual relations with a person other than your spouse, is a common exception chosen by many, but Jesus addressed that, too.

"You have heard the commandment that says, 'You must not commit adultery.' But I say, anyone who even looks at a woman with lust has already committed adultery with her in his heart." (Matthew 5:27-28)

Adultery is not a legitimate reason for divorce. Everyone— myself included—has committed adultery in one form or another, whether it's been physically, mentally, emotionally, or relationally. And all of us have committed adultery against God, spiritually, by our lusting after the things of this world, by not remaining faithful to him while he is always faithful to us. Our pride and our sin and our unfaithfulness is a foul stench in the nostrils of God; it's more than a miracle that he gave us his virgin Son. And we killed him!

But God forgave us. He forgave our cheating hearts. He forgives even our current sins. He traded the holiness of Jesus for the stink of man and he won't undo it—he doesn't break his promises. And he is our model. This is the path we follow if we claim to be born again, born out of this pattern of cheating and lying and whoring around with the ways of the world.

Our role, if we discover adultery, is to do what Jesus did with the woman caught in the act: forgive. Choosing not to forgive places us in the seat of God as judge, and we are not worthy. The unfaithfulness of a spouse does not negate our responsibility to remain faithful. Those who perform wedding ceremonies for divorced men and women essentially condone and promote adultery; and they severely limit the opportunity for reconciliation and healing by denying the power of God.

There are some married men and women who choose to draw a line in the sand, a line of conditions and offenses that, if crossed, removes the options of forgiveness, and restoration, and new life—oddly, they are all the things we gladly accept from Jesus but refuse to offer our spouses. It's not our responsibility to demand grace, but to give it. Over and over and over. The God who loves us with an everlasting love showed us the way to do it by sending Jesus, the clearest and most obvious example of sacrificial commitment.

So what happens now? If you're divorced, what do you do? Make every possible effort at reconciliation. If that's not possible, or while you try and wait, rely on the strength of your marriage to Jesus. The Bible says we are the bride of Christ, he is our groom. He will give you the wholeness you think you lack. There is no guarantee that an unfaithful spouse will return. And there is no point in arguing who is at fault; we are all sinners and as such can claim some responsibility. It's not always possible to avoid being the recipient of a divorce, but there is no good reason to add adultery to the long list of complications. Honoring God is our first priority and his eternal blessings will far outweigh any temporary pain.

If you have already remarried, what do you do now? You do what you do with any sin—you confess it; so together confess your sin. God already knows about it and is only waiting on you; forgiveness comes in the shape of Jesus. Begin your journey of spiritual maturity and make an unbreakable commitment now.

What if, contrary to all of the Scripture's teaching, you're still considering a divorce and remarriage and have decided that you'll find a replacement first and then confess your sin later? I strongly advise against playing games with God. Hebrews 10:26 says, "Dear friends, if we deliberately continue sinning after we have received knowledge of the truth, there is no longer any sacrifice that will cover these sins." God isn't interested in catering to your flesh desires, nor in being your second choice.

These are hard truths. My confession to you is this: There was a time in my marriage when things were so bad that it was unbearable, decades of pain and misery. I searched for two years to find a way out, a way to break the commitment that I had made before God and man, yet still have peace and his blessing. What you are reading are some of the verses God showed me; there were many others. It's been a long journey and my wife and I are finally turning the corner to reconciliation and a renewal of our first love, and he gets all the credit because it is indeed another miracle. And it has drawn me closer to him than I could have ever imagined. The entire matter is one of faithfulness regardless of circumstances. What God told me is that when I can find a place in the Scriptures where he gives up on me, then I can give up on her. It's not there.

Finding a good man

Q: Hello, I've been following your page and I have a question to ask. Why is it that most of us women find it hard to find a man who sees the qualities of a wife in us? Could it be that we have a bad character or we attract the wrong men? Why is it that a majority of God-fearing women are single and yet those who party and are worldly always end up with good marriages? Thanks and God bless.

A: Hi! Thanks for reading. Let me give you a couple verses before I reply; I want you to start thinking from a position of hope, not despair.

"Don't worry about the wicked or envy those who do wrong. For like grass, they soon fade away. Like spring flowers, they soon wither. Trust in the Lord and do good. Then you will live safely in the land and prosper." (Psalm 37:1-3)

First let's realize that what you see on the outside is rarely what's happening on the inside; these "good marriages" may or may not be good. No one will ever know the depths of the truth of what happens behind closed doors or in the mind and heart of an individual. In counseling I've seen people who are sharply different in private than what is seen by even their closest circle of friends and family. And this is true regardless of whether we're speaking of believers or unbelievers. So, as the verse says, don't envy them; you would likely find that you don't want what they have.

Second, you have an honorable desire, to have a godly man. How do you get one? I believe the fish you catch is strongly influenced by the type of bait you use on your hook. That's a bit of a shaky analogy, but please follow along. I want to give you another passage to help guide this conversation:

"I want women to be modest in their appearance. They should wear decent and appropriate clothing and not draw attention to themselves by the way they fix their hair or by wearing gold or pearls or expensive clothes. For women who claim to be devoted to God should make themselves attractive by the good things they do." (1 Timothy 2:9-10)

Every book you read or seminar you attend on the differences in the sexes will say the same primary thing about men: they are visually stimulated—they are attracted by the physical appearance of women. This should be no surprise and women know it based on the billions of dollars a year that they spend on clothes and makeup and jewelry and gym memberships and tanning salons and manicures and hair stylists. Men love beautiful women, and it's completely natural. But it must not stop there; do they love what's below the surface? This is why I believe Paul's counsel is so good. If you dress scantily or lower your standards you will only need to fish in the shallow water and what you catch you will almost always want to throw back.

Your pool of eligible candidates will shrink considerably if you seek a man who loves your body AND your heart and mind and soul. But this is your target. The time that I've spent counseling internationally has quickly proved that nearly all women everywhere want the same basic qualities, but few are willing to wait on a godly man or to choose no man if the godly pool is empty. Some want a child so bad they will simply take the first man who's willing to provide the necessary equipment to build one, of which there is never a shortage. Taking that path will accomplish the goal, but the result generally is a single mom and a fatherless child, both abandoned.

Another thought from Paul: "A woman who is no longer married or has never been married can be devoted to the Lord and holy in body and in spirit. But a married woman has to think about her earthly responsibilities and how to please her husband. I am saying this for your benefit, not to place restrictions on you. I want you to do whatever will help you serve the Lord best, with as few distractions as possible." (1 Corinthians 7:34-35)

I would encourage you to seek to please God first, and yourself second. If you go back to Genesis, God created Woman as the completer of Man, but he did not create her to be unequally yoked to an ungodly man. Nor did he create her to be used and abused by a man who doesn't hold her in the same esteem as does God. It's my personal belief that a holy marriage is the crown of God's creation and it's where both the male and female will discover wholeness, and it's where they will find the greatest possible satisfaction during this life. I pray God will bless you with the desires of your heart in such a way that you can honor him and experience his perfect peace and joy.

Predestination

Q: Good day sir, I just want to ask your opinion on whether it is us who makes our destiny, or is it God?

A: Be careful about asking for anyone's opinion, as each person thinks differently and from different bases of experience and history, and also sees things through different life filters. That's why I depend almost exclusively on the Bible, with only a couple of peeks here and there at commentaries and the viewpoints of a few other writers who have been able to stimulate my thought process, which I still take back to compare to Scripture because the Bible is the root of all wisdom and knowledge; its words come directly from the mouth of the one and only true and almighty God who created the universe and us. Slightly out of context—but it applies to his overall nature and this discussion so we need to remember it—is this verse: "God is not a God of disorder but of peace." (1 Corinthians 14:33)

The Old Testament is full of writers who declare that God determines the destiny of man. The New Testament talks about our freedom to choose, our free will. God has determined the destiny of those who are good or evil, which is heaven or hell. We get to choose which path we will take. But our free will falls inside the barriers of God's will. Otherwise we could just simply choose to believe that there isn't a God at all, and it would be so. Which isn't the case; even atheists have a belief that involves God. They strive to deny God. If they truly didn't believe God existed they wouldn't even give the subject another thought, but they can't run from his presence. Ecclesiastes 3:11 declares, "He has planted eternity in the human heart." And all of the other religions around the world acknowledge some higher power, even if it's the heightening of one's own knowledge and abilities, or nirvana, or something. So everyone has a sense of God, whether or not they want to admit it or name him. It must be exhausting to never stop running; I pray that those who haven't chosen his path will someday stop running from him so they can find rest before it's too late.

There are two paths from which we may choose. We are born on the one that leads to hell, and we will stay on it until we choose to follow Jesus on the path to heaven. And that takes a decision to recognize we are sinners and he is the cure. Trusting

Jesus is what changes our direction and our destiny. There is a lot of arguing in the church about predestination, but it is completely unnecessary and a distraction from more productive work. God cursed the world and man with death because of sin; we were predestined to hell from the very beginning. God also blessed the world and man with Jesus so we wouldn't have to suffer death; we were predestined to heaven if we elect to follow Jesus. It still comes down to a choice, but a choice that follows his guidelines.

Those who promote the idea that some people are predestined for one place or the other and have no choice over the matter don't seem to have a grasp of the entirety of Scripture. I know that's saying a lot because there are people with decades of education and multiple degrees and high positions of authority, and even centuries-old denominations, that believe this. But take Pharaoh and the plagues in Egypt: in Exodus 10:1 the Lord told Moses, "I have made him and his officials stubborn so I can display my miraculous signs among them." You can say this is an instance of God planning the demise of man, predestining him for failure. But in the preceding chapters Pharaoh is recorded as having yielded to God's commands through Moses, then reverting to his "stubborn" or "hard-hearted" nature (depending on which translation you read) whenever God gave him relief from the plagues. The fact that there wasn't permanent damage to his authority or kingdom in the initial stages of these events caused him to fall back into his pattern of pride and disobedience. What had made Pharaoh hard-hearted was God's power yet mercy, and it was his choice to be grateful or hateful. When the last plague took Pharaoh's firstborn son, he finally released the Hebrews from slavery. But shortly afterward he became even angrier and more stubborn and chased them through the desert and into the Red Sea where he was drowned, along with his whole army.

In my example a few days ago of my near-accident in the car while traveling with my wife, and the fact that we escaped without injury or mishap, I quoted Job 23:14: "So he will do to me whatever he has planned. He controls my destiny." To continue that discussion, let's add a couple more thoughts. God controlled my destiny by giving me all the tools necessary to succeed; how I used them, or if I used them, is up to me. I could have been drunk and not able to react quickly enough. I could have been irresponsible and not maintained my vehicle. I could have been belligerent and refused to move out of the way of the other cars. Any of those changes would have caused a much different outcome. God can do anything, but he gives us the freedom to choose and it impacts the way he responds.

Compare Pharaoh to Job. Job had everything taken from him —all of his children!—but his heart was humble and dedicated to God. Even after his wife bitterly challenged him to give up, to curse God and die, he remained humble and replied to her, "Should we accept only good things from the hand of God and never anything bad?" And he was blessed many times over. In the New Testament we have Judas betraying Jesus and then trying to undo his dark deed by renegotiating with the religious leaders who had paid him. It didn't work, but instead of going to Jesus and confessing, he becoming so overwrought with his guilt that he committed suicide. Peter denied Jesus three times but humbled himself and returned to serve him; eventually he wrote two books of the Bible and Jesus used him to "build my church" (Matthew 16:18). Who would have ever guessed? But it was in the hearts of these men to refuse or yield, to deny or accept. Both were disciples, both knew the same Jesus, but with two totally different outcomes. Every human has this option. We get caught up in thinking we know enough to know everything, but that puts us into the place of God, a place we don't belong. He is not restricted by time or space. He is in the past and the present and the future—at the same time! In Exodus 8:15 after Pharaoh decided to change his mind about freeing the slaves and had become rebellious again, the verse ends with, "just as the Lord had predicted." And because Jesus (who is God) knew how Judas would respond when he was "prompted" by the devil, he told him at the Passover supper to, "Hurry and do what you're going to do." (John 13:2, 27)

God is going to use everyone and everything to bring glory to his name and it's up to us to decide how we want to be remembered in eternity, as a help or a hindrance. Jesus said two very critically important things in John 3:17-18: "God sent his Son into the world not to judge the world, but to save the world" because "anyone who does not believe in him has already been judged for not believing." Our default position, the default position of all of mankind, because of sin, is disbelief and judgment and destruction and hell. We can alter that destination only by believing, by making a choice to follow Jesus instead of our rebellious and stubborn natural predisposition. Let's use that word instead—predisposition—because predestination, although taken from the words "predestined" and "predestinate" and "predestinated" in the Bible, has become a whole belief system in itself and is being misinterpreted to mean some people don't have a choice. Mankind was created to worship God; mankind was created in the image of God. He knows who will choose to surrender to him and who won't. We do not know, so it is still our responsibility to continue to share the message of salvation.

To take the religion of predestination to its conclusion would mean there is no reason at all to care about anyone else's future because God already has it resolved. I don't see any place in Scripture that says we should find a couch to sit by and watch. We are still humans and God is God and we must obey: Jesus came to spread the message of hope and life—and he knows the future—so we must do what he did. Everyone has a choice until their last breath. We can take the final word from 2 Peter 3:9 where he tells us that God "does not want anyone to be destroyed, but wants everyone to repent."

Suicide

Q: What happens when Christians want to commit suicide? You must think it's a silly question.

A: No, not silly; that's a good question. First I have to think about the definition of a Christian: Christians are people who trust in Jesus for their salvation from sin. That means confessing that they are sinners and need salvation in the first place. Once someone surrenders to God by claiming Jesus' sacrifice on the cross as their payment for sin, the Holy Spirit comes to "convict of sin, of righteousness, and of judgment." With the Holy Spirit's guidance one can find hope and joy in any situation.

So how does a Christian even consider suicide? How can hopelessness come into the picture? The only answer I can imagine is the scenario in which a person never really surrendered to God. Everywhere in the Bible God says, "I will never leave you." "Do not be afraid." "Trust me." Suicide

42

conflicts with all of those statements. Can someone be mentally ill and lose control of their thinking and choices? Of course that's possible; sin comes in all shapes and sizes. In that case, God will decide whether their decisions were valid or authentic, or not. I think of infants who die and never had a chance to reason or choose. I believe God saves them.

So does a mentally ill person fall into that category? My answer would be, yes. But there are people who choose suicide as a rebellion against submission or as an escape from dealing responsibly with life's difficulties or refusing to turn them over to the Lord. I don't know that those people have a chance with God if they reject him; but wouldn't rejection of God be the same as a mental illness? That would cover a lot of people.

The real bottom line, though, is that no one knows the heart of a person except God. Even in the milliseconds of life before it ends, what is God doing? Is he intensely involved in the heart and mind of that person as they are getting ready to meet him? The Bible talks about a day being like a thousand years to God and a thousand years like a day. So a few seconds could be more than enough time for him to say to the dying person, "Really? Is this what you want?" Your own decision is the only one you will ever know. Everyone will answer on their own to him, just like you will.

If you are considering suicide, please ask for help. Pray to God for relief from whatever is clouding your thinking; seek his hand because he will never let go of yours. If you have lost someone to suicide don't assume that God was finished with them; we will know in eternity what was really going on and, miraculously, it will make perfect sense because we will have knowledge there that was impossible to have here. Above all, trust God that he knows what he is doing, he loves you, and your life is a treasure to him.

Depression

The rate of suicides across all demographics seems to be rising at a time when there are more resources than ever available for mental health treatment. I don't think anyone is immune from the feelings of discouragement and depression that may lead to thoughts of suicide, but we may be starting at the wrong place in our war to fight it. This is a personal response to the previous discussion, so please process it accordingly.

*****

"I am losing all hope; I am paralyzed with fear . . . come quickly, Lord, and answer me, for my depression deepens. Don't turn away from me, or I will die." (Psalms 143:4, 7)

It's terrible to see the loss of someone young and beautiful or popular and talented; but I'm sure it's equally terrible to lose someone ugly—or who perceives that he or she is ugly.

I was 14 years old, walking down the hallway between classes in middle school feeling pretty miserable about my life, when I heard a voice. As you know, peer pressure at that point in the life of a young person is extreme. In the throes of puberty and the mental anguish that comes with trying to figure out who you want to be when you "grow up," no youth feels acceptable or liked, regardless of their surroundings, position, or appearance. (I actually think that struggle continues forever until you get the answer.) Feeling like a total dork, awkward in most ways and with braces and zits, believing everything bad that was said about me or done to me—I was a loser. But I remember vividly, even now, God speaking to me in the midst of all the noise. "It doesn't matter what anyone else thinks about you; it matters what I think. I created you. I planned you and designed you and you are beautiful to me."

It was a turning point in my life. I'm sure that chemical imbalances play a part in the causes of depression and personality disorders because we are complex beings. But they play only a part; instead, I would credit many of the problems we experience to understanding imbalances. God usually only gets a footnote when it comes to treatment solutions if he gets even that much of an acknowledgement, but he is the Creator of mankind—and he is certainly capable of fixing his creation. Maybe we could start there instead of leaving him as the option of last resort. If we were created in his image, then we can respond to our trials like he did and still does.

Most cases of depression with which I'm familiar include heavy doses of negative external influences. The ill effects of peer pressure aren't limited to youth nor are the obvious violations of trust that come with all types of physical and mental abuse. Some cases start in youth, but some are new events by new violators. Science has proven that the way we think impacts the way we feel. And how we feel impacts our physical and mental health, even down to the level of internal chemical changes. God created us for good relationships—with him and with our fellow man. When they break down, we break down.

Let's look at Jesus, because his example is the one we are encouraged to model. What did he do when his trust was violated? When he was let down? When he was abused? Seems like somewhere there is a story about him hanging naked on a cross, scourged and bloody, his shoulders and back sticking to the rough wood, fastened in place with spikes in his hands and feet, the soldiers' spit dripping down his face over the fresh bruises they had given him. Enduring the mocking and ridicule of his own people. Seeing his mother weep as she watched him die. And he said, "Father forgive them, for they don't know what they're doing."

I would suggest this as a starting point to healing: Look at the people who have hurt you, but look at them through God's eyes. They are on the same path of life that you are. More likely they've slipped off the path, but they're lost and stumbling like you used to be, and they're trying to find it. As much as their abuse seems personal, it's more a violent outpouring of their own mess than it is a personal attack. I don't say that to excuse it, just to partly explain it; no one in their right mind willfully harms another person. You may feel a need to remove yourself from life-threatening relationships, but offer forgiveness to those involved, even if it's only in your own mind, and turn to your Creator for the wholeness and affirmation that you may have unknowingly looked for in others. He's the only one who will ever love you completely and without condemnation—even with all your bumps and bruises. And he will immediately forgive you for looking elsewhere as he welcomes you into his arms. And healing will begin.

It worked for me.

Which day is the Sabbath?

Q: Why do we have Sabbath on Sunday when scripture suggest Sabbath is on Saturday. I have done research on this and I am really thinking that the Sabbath is Saturday. What are your thoughts?

A: Our Judeo-Christian calendar week starts on Sunday which would indicate Saturday is the end of the week, or the "day of rest." I think the technicality is less important than the functionality. God wants us to take a day out of our work week to rest and reflect; that's what he did when he finished creating the world. "God blessed the seventh day and declared it holy, because it was the day when he rested from all his work of creation" (Genesis 2:3).

The idea of it being a worship day is man-made. We should worship God every day. And fellowship with other believers shouldn't be restricted to one formal meeting per week. The irony of our current-day practice is that the ones preaching the sanctity of the Sabbath are the ones working on it. Double irony is that everyone crowds into a restaurant after the service expecting it to be open for business and filled with workers. I doubt the silliness escapes God.

Jesus talked about this hangup with "the rules" when he healed a man on the Sabbath and the religious leaders who were present implied that he—Jesus!—was sinning. And another time when he and the disciples were walking through a wheat field, the Pharisees derided the disciples for taking grains off the stalks and eating them, harvesting—"working"—on the Sabbath.

Jesus said, "The Sabbath was made to meet the needs of people, and not people to meet the requirements of the Sabbath." (Mark 2:27)

What is the benefit of dating?

Q: What is the benefit of dating?

A: It depends on what you mean by dating. Social interaction is good for getting to know another's interests, to know how the other responds to different stimuli, what's funny, what's sad, whether salad or steak or ice cream is preferred. Do they like to read or sing or dance? But dating that includes expensive activities in which one or the other feels obligated to repay in some manner adds significant tension. Sexual activity is always a burden that can never be satisfactorily addressed as it puts both people in a position to have to perform one way or another and under significant pressure. And it breaks a spiritual bond that can't be rebuilt without God.

I recommend group socialization, not being in a place where the opportunity to sin presents itself. If you really think you found the right one, make a commitment. Get married. Pledge to work out the differences that will undoubtedly come up. In a casual relationship that doesn't include a marriage commitment you will never really get to know the person with whom you will one day face a terrible conflict. Decide now that you won't let it tear you apart. Satan loves to ruin marriages. Don't let him win by giving in to separation and divorce.

Q: How can dating help someone to develop their personality?

A: Social interaction of any kind is helpful in developing who you are. Learning that there are other perspectives, other ways of thinking, expands your own mind. God created us for community, not isolation. There is no way one person, with the limits we have on our time and energy, can be as productive as a couple or group or team. And listening is as important, if not more important, than speaking.

Backsliding . . . again!

Q: I'm backsliding and I need help. I don't know how to get out of the pit again! The Lord did a mighty work in restoring me and here I am again in the same spot. Don't even want sweet words I just want repentance and for the Lord to tell me he never left me, you know? And it seems like the Lord has been very silent so I'm not sure what he thinks of this. I know he doesn't take sin lightly and so I've been praying for him to cleanse my heart and discipline me. Just haven't heard much of him and I never know what to think, so it gets hard to get back up and press on.

A: Okay. I've been thinking and praying about your comments. There is no way I can know what you're going through but I do know what God goes through as he watches since he tells us in his Word. He loves you. But I'll cut to the chase: Jesus already suffered any punishment you might think you deserve. And, frankly, you or I couldn't survive what we deserve which is why Jesus had to take it. But I'm guessing the silence you are sensing is God waiting on you to turn back to him—for real this time. If you've slipped back into the same sins from which he already rescued you, you have enough knowledge of him to know better. Stand up, turn around, and walk toward him. Today, right now. I'm thinking of the story in Genesis 19 where Lot's wife looked back longingly at the evil city God was destroying and she turned into a pillar of salt; God had told her not to look back! But she loved her past more than she respected his power or trusted him with the future. You have everything you need to make the turn. God loves you; Jesus isn't going to the cross again; you are already a new creation—so be new. And I love you as my brother in the Lord.

Q: Thank you brother! I've actually been thinking and praying as well and I know that James tells us to draw near to God and he will draw near to us, so that's what I'm gonna do until he answers me. Oddly enough I thought it was some sort of harsh discipline that would break me, but it's his silence that kills me.

A: Beautiful perspective! A true relationship is felt most intensely when it's missing. That's probably what the person meant who framed the original quote of "absence makes the heart grow fonder." Too bad that we always have to find out the hard way.

Q: That's definitely true! So just one more issue; obviously the consequences of sin is a hardened heart, and to keep it real that describes me. Do you think God can restore or would that be too far gone?

A: Your view of God is too small. But the disciples had the same problem and they lived with Jesus every day. Read these verses:

"The disciples were astounded. 'Then who in the world can be saved?' they asked. Jesus looked at them intently and said, 'Humanly speaking, it is impossible. But with God everything is possible.'" (Matthew 19:25-26)

"But you must remain faithful to the things you have been taught. You know they are true, for you know you can trust those who taught you." (2 Timothy 3:14)

"So humble yourselves before God. Resist the devil, and he will flee from you." (James 4:7)

Following Jesus is the hardest decision you'll ever make. But the reward is the greatest and he gives us the Holy Spirit to help with discernment and strength. Submitting is way harder than being prideful. And if you think you've done something that can't be forgiven, that's pride. And it's wrong. Everything is possible with God.

Q: Thank you brother for your encouragement. I guess that's what continual sin does! I'm grateful that I'm coming to my senses.

Does religion help us?

Q: How does religion explain man's experience and what is its role in their lives?

A: The first thing I would share with you is that religion has no place in Christianity. Religion is simply ritual; Christianity is a relationship. It's the reason I believe in God and the sacrifice of his Son, versus something else. All other religions in the world require some kind of actions or adherence to a set of ways to become holy or find peace. Instead, God brought holiness and peace to us in the way of his Son, Jesus—he did all the work, not us, and we just have to trust him—totally different from religion. God created man for relationship. In Genesis you'll see the Lord coming to walk and talk with Adam and Eve in the Garden in the cool of the evening—that's relational, not dictatorial or authoritarian. He sacrificed everything to reach across time and space to restore our relationship with him.

No other "religion" even comes close to something that would appeal to the thinking person. God gave us brains and he permits us to reason out our belief. It's not blind faith that we have, but reasoned and calculated faith—faith without seeing, but not faith without knowing. Our faith in God and his plan is a surety we can have and it's confirmed by the presence of the Holy Spirit who dwells in the one who believes. Our role in this world and this life is to reflect his love of us in the way we love him back and the way we love others. It may be hard at times because the enemy attacks us, but that only refines and purifies our belief like fire does to gold.

We must confess that we are sinners in need of a Savior, which the Bible talks about extensively, but that is obvious to anyone who is honest with themselves. No person, in the solitude of darkness in bed in the middle of the night, can believe that he or she is totally good and sinless. Jesus is that Savior. No other religion offers Jesus. It makes me want to jump out of my skin with joy!

Q: What do you make of this passage in Matthew 11:16-19? I don't understand it:

"To what can I compare this generation? It is like children playing a game in the public square. They complain to their friends,

'We played wedding songs,
and you didn't dance,
so we played funeral songs,
and you didn't mourn.'

For John didn't spend his time eating and drinking, and you say, 'He's possessed by a demon.' The Son of Man, on the other hand, feasts and drinks, and you say, 'He's a glutton and a drunkard, and a friend of tax collectors and other sinners!' But wisdom is shown to be right by its results."

A: I believe Jesus is speaking to the childish whimsical nature of people who aren't pleased with any style of preaching so they listen to none. John the Baptist was a rough austere figure living in the wilderness living off of a diet of locusts and honey, and Jesus walked with the people eating and drinking; the crowd wouldn't listen to either one of them. Very much like current day listeners: nitpick the messenger so you can deny the message. Or only listen as long as you are entertained.

Tithes and Offerings

Q: Hello! Do you have any thoughts regarding tithes in today's times? We are Christians, but we don't attend church due to too many instances of evil pastors in our lives. I'm exploring the topic of tithing to learn the truth instead of feeling guilty if I don't send my money to a church (as I was "trained" by all those pastors).

A: The original design of the formal tithe was to provide for the Levites who were assigned to care for the Temple and who served as priests to offer sacrifices for the people; the other tribes contributed one-tenth of their produce and flocks to support them.

But modern times: Jesus was the final sacrifice on the cross and the Holy Spirit now comes to live in us—we are the temple of God. Buildings and properties and staff and complicated religious organizations are not required for us to worship God, which he says we must do in spirit and in truth. When money or the things money can buy become the central focus of ministry, ministry breaks down. Jesus, even before his crucifixion and resurrection, had plenty of harsh words for the religious leaders of his day whose primary goal seemed to be the enslavement of the very people he came to set free.

So, technically and biblically, there is no direction to contribute a tithe today. However, offerings are a completely different matter. Proverbs 3:9 says, "Honor the Lord with your wealth and with the best part of everything you produce." Yes, that is Old Testament, but it matches with what Jesus commands us to do in the New Testament: "You must love the Lord your God with all your heart, all your soul, and all your mind." He wants considerably more than ten percent—he wants all of us!

Other Scripture commands us to give the "first fruits" of what we earn, and to give the best of what we have to God. It tells us multiple places to provide for orphans, foreigners, widows, children, etc. Regardless of which section of the Bible you choose, you will see a God who models generosity and sacrificial giving—the life of Jesus cost him much more than the equivalent of a simple tithe or offering.

To attempt to undo what may have been bad teaching or misdirection, I will suggest to you that you recognize God as the source of every talent, skill, or good idea that you have; he is the one who gives you breath and a heartbeat and life; he is the one who offers hope and joy and peace. To give to him or to contribute to what he is doing is something that will bring you extraordinary satisfaction and it is the type of obedience for which he will reward you in blessings that far exceed your gift.

Don't get too caught up in whether we deal with Old or New Testament to find the right counsel: God is the same God throughout all of time. Malachi is the prophet in the last book of the Old Testament and he offered a challenge; to those who are selfish or try to cheat God by withholding what he wants them to give (which is ultimately 100%, not 10%) he says this from the mouth of God: "Bring all the tithes into the storehouse so there will be enough food in my Temple. If you do, I will open the windows of heaven for you. I will pour out a blessing so great you won't have enough room to take it in! Try it! Put me to the test!"

The challenge is really less about the mechanics of giving and more about the condition of the heart. Pray about it. Ask God to show you where you should put your offerings. I don't believe it's necessary to pay for buildings and weekly gatherings unless you participate in them and feel it is something you wish to support. But there are endless needs out there for which God has blessed you with the ability and resources to meet. And you can't out-give him, so if you are to believe Malachi, get a bigger wallet!

Honorable Male/Female relationships

Q: Hi sir. Can you please tell me how one can develop a godly relationship between boyfriend and girlfriend, and what principles should it be based on. List them if possible. Thank you in advance.

A: Okay, here are some thoughts, not necessarily in any order of importance as they are all components of a relationship that will flourish and honor God:

1.) "Don't team up with those who are unbelievers. How can righteousness be a partner with wickedness? How can light live with darkness?" (2 Corinthians 6:14)

Don't even begin thinking of a serious relationship unless you both are committed to Christ. You can't start in blatant disobedience and expect success.

2.) "She is your equal partner in God's gift of new life. Treat her as you should so your prayers will not be hindered." (1 Peter 3:7b)

Neither of you must go into the relationship with a position of superiority or inferiority. God created you both with perfection and glory in mind. Work together to discover his plan for you as individuals and as a couple; you complement each other and make the "one flesh" union a model of the oneness of the Father, Son, and Holy Spirit.

3.) "And further, submit to one another out of reverence for Christ." (Ephesians 5:21)

Your goals are to lift each other up. Always be on the lookout for ways to invest in the emotional, spiritual, physical, and mental well-being of the other.

4.) "Don't be concerned for your own good but for the good of others." (1 Corinthians 10:24)

There will be times when one or the other of you is in the depths of despair or pain or selfishness. That's when you have to rise up and be holy, be Christlike. Loving unconditionally is the key to being a Christian and even more critical in a marriage as it is the most intimate connection you will ever have.

5.) "'This explains why a man leaves his father and mother and is joined to his wife, and the two are united into one.' Since they are no longer two but one, let no one split apart what God has joined together." (Mark 10:7-9)

Intentionally decide to remain committed no matter what. Fidelity is the heart of God. He never leaves us and never gives up on us even though we constantly fail him. Pledge to honor the relationship more highly than the people in the relationship. Expect occasional failures because we are only human. God gives us the power to forgive and restore brokenness. Use his power.

6.) "Dear friends, let us continue to love one another, for love comes from God. Anyone who loves is a child of God and knows God. But anyone who does not love does not know God, for God is love." (1 John 4:7-8)

Lean on God for your strength and fulfillment. You are a spiritual being permanently, and a physical being temporarily. No other person can complete your spirit, only the one who made you can do that. Rely on him for everything.

Masturbation

Q: What is your biblical take on masturbation?

A: That's a good one. Give me some time to put together a thorough response.

*****

True confession: This question is almost five months old. With my recent series involving sex and godliness, it has been asked more times, by both women and men, and I'm still dragging my feet. So I apologize to those who have asked and to those who haven't asked but may be wondering. It's a difficult question because of its very personal nature, which makes it uncomfortable to discuss, and historically it's been dealt with poorly by the church. I've done quite a bit of reading in anticipation of having to eventually answer this question and the writers I've come across have only provided awkward, embarrassing, and incomplete responses. So, is masturbation right or wrong? If we're completely honest—which is always the goal of my counsel, to develop open and honest dialogue—none of us are qualified to judge; and God is the only judge who matters anyway. But I don't think the answer is nearly as complicated as we make it.

"Run from sexual sin! No other sin so clearly affects the body as this one does. For sexual immorality is a sin against your own body. Don't you realize that your body is the temple of the Holy Spirit, who lives in you and was given to you by God? You do not belong to yourself, for God bought you with a high price. So you must honor God with your body." (1 Corinthians 6:18-20)

God created the human body; he is an amazing Creator and nothing is bad about it or wrong with the way any of its senses interact with each other. The human body is many things: physical, emotional, spiritual, relational, psychological, and sexual. The Bible does not say sexuality is a sin, but sexual immorality is a sin. What is immorality? Immorality is conduct that is harmful or evil or wicked. As a Christian "you do not belong to yourself" so you must honor the owner, who is God. What could make sexuality immoral? It is the state of the mind or heart.

"But I say, anyone who even looks at a woman with lust has already committed adultery with her in his heart." (Matthew 5:28)

Jesus is talking about marriage and fidelity, but his view addresses the state of the mind and heart. Lust is described as an intense, overpowering, uncontrolled desire, often connected to sexual craving but easily applied to other appetites such as wealth, power, food, attention, and so on. I know men who lust after cars and women who lust after shoes. It's the condition of a mind that wants to be filled with joy that comes from something other than the Lord. Paul writes about not being drunk with wine but with the Spirit of God. If you're going to be overcome with something, let it be with godliness.

Masturbation is defined as the manipulation or stimulation of the genitals, by a method other than sexual intercourse, to the point of orgasm—meaning your own or another's. I mention this because the subject is usually discussed as a personal, self-gratifying event, but it should not be removed from the context of marriage because science and research indicates that less than 10 percent of women are able to reach orgasm by sexual intercourse only, whereas men achieve it almost 100 percent of the time. So it's irresponsible to ignore in our discussion its proper application within the bounds of a healthy marriage relationship, as it would be to the obvious advantage of the woman and the happiness of the man who wants his wife to be satisfied.

As it relates personally: What is the motive? As initially stated, the body is sexual. Hormones exist and they often act independently of the bearer; the case of orgasms occurring while sleeping or in other states of unconsciousness is not debated and are not the product of an intentional act either moral or immoral. Both men and women experience instances of needing to release sexual tension for various and sundry reasons, many that are not ungodly. Therefore, this is something that should be taken to the Lord. That is not an evasive or simplistic answer; he is the one who made your body and he is the one who can help.

Some of the reading I've done lists all kinds of actual situations with pre-programmed remedies, but there is no way to cover every contingency without likely excluding the specific one that is burdening you, so in my opinion it's foolish to attempt it; God is not absent or inaccessible to his children and he eagerly desires to hear the concerns of your heart. If you are engaged in masturbation for dishonorable reasons it will be clear when you talk to him. He is not going to give you his blessing to lust after a person to whom you are not married. He is not going to bless activity that becomes addictive or obsessive. He is not going to bless you if you are bored or lazy or selfish or angry. He is not going to encourage any actions that will harm you, your spouse, or anyone else. As long as you search for answers from men, you won't ask God; and you will likely get what you're looking for instead of what he has to give you.

God did not make you an extraordinary and complex being and then deny you the freedom of discovery. He did not create you for guilt and shame. Because of Jesus you are perfect in his eyes, and he is making you holy. It's a process in which he takes great pleasure and invites your full participation.

"Create in me a clean heart, O God. Renew a loyal spirit within me." (Psalms 51:10)

Could God change his mind about me?

Q: I'm sorry for bothering you like this. How can I avoid this being said to me by the Lord: I never knew you; depart from me?

A: Here's the passage; it pays to read these words from Jesus in context: "Beware of false prophets who come disguised as harmless sheep but are really vicious wolves. You can identify them by their fruit, that is, by the way they act. Can you pick grapes from thornbushes, or figs from thistles? A good tree produces good fruit, and a bad tree produces bad fruit. A good tree can't produce bad fruit, and a bad tree can't produce good fruit. So every tree that does not produce good fruit is chopped down and thrown into the fire. Yes, just as you can identify a tree by its fruit, so you can identify people by their actions. Not everyone who calls out to me, 'Lord! Lord!' will enter the Kingdom of Heaven. Only those who actually do the will of my Father in heaven will enter. On judgment day many will say to me, 'Lord! Lord! We prophesied in your name and cast out demons in your name and performed many miracles in your name.' But I will reply, 'I never knew you. Get away from me, you who break God's laws.'" (Matthew 7:15-23)

Jesus spent a lot of time warning the people against the corrupt religious leaders. They would make hard rules and then not follow them themselves. He modeled a life of loving and forgiving, not making impossible rules. Surrendering your will to the Father's will might sound impossible to the one who is proud and resistant. But that is the first and only real challenge to our sinful natures. Your true condition before God will be evident by how you strive to be like Jesus. But he also knows we are weak, which is why he sent his Holy Spirit.

"And this is the will of God, that I should not lose even one of all those he has given me, but that I should raise them up at the last day." (John 6:39)

Q: So when I keep the laws that God has given us to obey then the Lord won't say that to me? And what commands am I supposed to follow, the Ten Commandments and what else?

A: Don't get strangled by trying to be perfect. You can't do it. Read this answer to the religious leaders who asked which commandment was most important: "Jesus replied, 'You must love the Lord your God with all your heart, all your soul, and all your mind.' This is the first and greatest commandment. A second is equally important: 'Love your neighbor as yourself.' The entire law and all the demands of the prophets are based on these two commandments.'" (Matthew 22:37-40)

If you are trusting in Jesus' death on the cross as the payment for your sins, there is no higher price that can be paid.

Love God and love your neighbor. But whether you fail in following one thing or a million things you can't uncrucify Jesus. And God's power to raise him (and us) from the dead and grant eternal life isn't somehow restricted or weakened because we are weak. Think of us the way the Bible identifies us, as the children of God. No good father would ever reject his children, even when they don't measure up to his hopes for them. That's why he had to give us Jesus to pick us up where we don't succeed.

Raising godly children

Q: How do I get my kids more involved with God?

A: Wow, that is maybe the most important question of a parent's life. I still struggle with it even though my kids are fully grown and have their own kids. And the importance of it strikes me again. I think of Adam and Eve and their two boys; they each took entirely different paths and probably had the exact same upbringing.

My recommendation, when they are young, is to read to them. I remember Bible stories my mom read to me, and they still stand out to me when I read them now. They were very formative at such a young age when the world was new and everything was followed by a question mark. God pleads with his people to follow his commands and know his ways. In Deuteronomy 6:7 he says, "Repeat them again and again to your children. Talk about them when you are at home and when you are on the road, when you are going to bed and when you are getting up." As they get older, the biggest lesson you can offer them is your own modeling. How they see you love God will dictate to them how real he is. Many people live a fraudulent life, faking it for the people who know them outside the home. But those who are living inside the doors, the ones who see the genuine person, know the truth. And your words will mean nothing if your actions don't match them.

When they are old enough to be making their own decisions away from your presence, your conduct still matters, but that's when you really have to trust them to God. Not that you shouldn't be trusting him the whole time, but when you no longer have frequent physical contact or emotional connection, it's harder. Proverbs 22:6 says, "Direct your children onto the right path, and when they are older, they will not leave it." It's incredibly difficult to trust God when you know what's right and see them doing what's wrong. But you can't let worry or anxiety eat you because it will. There's a point where I had to recognize that God loves my kids even more than I do—he created them! And he is the only one who can always be with them and influence them.

I think the whole child-bearing/child-raising process, which continues until we no longer have breath, is designed to help us see the heart of God; how he loves us and wishes for us to "turn out right" and how it pains him when we step off the path.

I don't know enough about you to say what I'm going to say next, but it's true regardless: if you're married, follow God's plans for a healthy marriage. Wives are supposed to submit to their husbands, husbands are supposed to sacrificially love their wives—both are supposed to submit to each other as Christ has done for his church (read Ephesians 5). It's more complicated if one or both aren't playing fair or willfully disobey God. But that doesn't change the rules. Jesus loved us all the way to the cross. That is the model and that is what your kids need to see.

Baptism

Q: My question is, what if you were baptized before and slipped away but then returned to the Lord. Is it a must to be baptized again?

A: Short answer: No. Longer answer: Baptism is a public profession of your faith. I know people who've been baptized but don't even believe in God—they did it because their friends did it and they wanted to fit in with that group. It's only trust in Jesus that saves you. There are people who say that they trust Jesus, but it seems like a lie based on their actions and lifestyles. Only God knows what a person truly believes. The point is to live a life that demonstrates your belief; it's going to be evident to everyone around you what you really believe. I call it "life baptism" as an illustration that you should look new and alive compared to an old life of sin and disbelief.

This verse confuses some people: "Anyone who believes and is baptized will be saved. But anyone who refuses to believe will be condemned" (Mark 16:16). You don't have to be baptized to be saved. A lot of churches preach this and it's wrong because that's not what Jesus was saying. Believing in Jesus and trusting that his sacrifice on the cross paid for your sins and makes you right with God is what saves you. In fact, in the first chapter of Mark it says, "John the Baptist was in the wilderness and preached that people should be baptized to show that they had repented of their sins and turned to God to be forgiven." Baptism is a demonstration that you've turned away from sin, that you've changed sides. That's why we are called "Christians"—followers of Jesus Christ. And Christ isn't his last name; it is his title, meaning the Messiah or Deliverer. Jesus the Messiah has rescued us and delivered us from the penalty of sin, which is eternal death and damnation.

However the importance of baptism can't be overstated. Jesus said, "Everyone who acknowledges me publicly here on earth, I will also acknowledge before my Father in heaven. But everyone who denies me here on earth, I will also deny before my Father in heaven" (Matthew 10:32-33). Those words may have been why Peter was so distraught when he realized that he had three times denied knowing Jesus during his arrest and trial (that situation was rectified later between Jesus and Peter and he was forgiven).

If you say you are a Christian but are embarrassed to have anyone know it, or refuse to live as one, then you are not a Christian; the Holy Spirit has given us all the power we need to live boldly in our belief. Baptism should be part of the identity of any believer who is active and aware. Baptisms usually happen in small ceremonies, though, so it's not really going to serve well as a loudspeaker announcing your intentions or relationship. Your life should do that. People shouldn't be surprised to discover your allegiance to God.

I want to say it one more time: Trusting Jesus saves you, not baptism; otherwise the thief on the cross could never have hoped to see the paradise Jesus promised him. Baptism is a symbol of dying to sin, being buried, and God raising you again, new and clean. Water baptism is obedience, life baptism is evidence.

Q: That's my belief, too. Do I have to do it every time I want to become a Church member?

A: Some religious organizations may require it but it's not something God requires. The church, according to Jesus, is the people of God; it's not a building or a business or a brand name.

Sin in the Church

Q: I read what you wrote about divorce and what the Bible says. Recently I was thinking of leaving my marriage because of infidelity. The lady my husband was going out with has made my life a living hell and we are from the same church. I'm still hoping God will clear the issue and I look to have the God-fearing husband I once had. But again, I strongly feel I should leave. Remember my family in your prayers.

A: I appreciate your vulnerability in sharing this very difficult problem. I want to reply to you based on one part of your comment: "we are from the same church." The Church is the body of Christ and we all have a responsibility to live honorably, obediently, and in a way that best serves the other members of the body. I don't know what your culture or community says about this kind of activity, but I do know what God says about it. Let me share a little piece of what Paul said when he wrote to the church in Corinth about similar sexual and relational sins that were discovered, and about which the leadership was choosing to look the other way instead of deal with them: "You are so proud of yourselves, but you should be mourning in sorrow and shame. And you should remove this man from your fellowship." (1 Corinthians 5:2)

The counsel the Bible gives us on fidelity and commitment and love and forgiveness does not forgo disciplinary measures to be taken when a part of the body is failing. When our natural body is sick or broken, we take steps to heal it. It's no different with our spiritual bodies or the body of Christ. Ignoring sin is the same as approving of it, and then it grows and infects the rest of the body. "Don't you realize that this sin is like a little yeast that spreads through the whole batch of dough?"

The responsibility of your church leadership is to confront your husband and this woman. This likely means you will have to start the conversation if it's happening right under their noses and nothing is being done about it. Paul goes on to say, "When I wrote to you before, I told you not to associate with people who indulge in sexual sin. But I wasn't talking about unbelievers . . . I meant that you are not to associate with anyone who claims to be a believer yet indulges in sexual sin."

God gives his children enough wisdom and direction to self-police and keep the temple clean and holy. "It isn't my responsibility to judge outsiders, but it certainly is your responsibility to judge those inside the church who are sinning. God will judge those on the outside; but as the Scriptures say, 'You must remove the evil person from among you.'"

Removal from fellowship is not permanent if the offenders acknowledge the sin and turn from their wicked ways. With repentance comes forgiveness and restoration to the body, but permitting sin to go on in the church brings shame on it and we become fools in the eyes of the same world we are trying to impact. Your role is to remain faithful and wait on the Lord; there is nothing harder than living in constant pain—but he will give you the strength to persevere and will draw you nearer as you seek him.

Dear God, please bless my sister and her husband. If there are children, shield them from this crisis that could wrongly shape their view of holy marriage; protect them. Bless this lady who is involved, Lord, that she would see the error of blatantly sinning before you. Bring correction and healing. Bless the leaders, help them to lead as you would. Lord, most of all I pray that you would turn this situation into one that brings glory to your name, healing to this family, and holiness to the body of Christ. In the mighty name of Jesus, Amen.

Spiritual Gifts

Q: How can you discover your gift or calling as a Christian?

A: Start by reading the fruits of the Holy Spirit as described in Galatians 5:22-23: "But the Holy Spirit produces this kind of fruit in our lives: love, joy, peace, patience, kindness, goodness, faithfulness, gentleness, and self-control. There is no law against these things!" You have all of these fruits as a believer, but one or two may seem to stand out stronger in you than others. See how you can apply them to your skills and talents, and how they match with your heart's desires. God made each of us uniquely with different qualities and characteristics. Likely the things that appeal to you are the parts of your gifting that God specifically put in you.

Then look at the list of gifts Paul itemizes in Romans 12:6-8: "In his grace, God has given us different gifts for doing certain things well. So if God has given you the ability to prophesy, speak out with as much faith as God has given you. If your gift is serving others, serve them well. If you are a teacher, teach well. If your gift is to encourage others, be encouraging. If it is giving, give generously. If God has given you leadership ability, take the responsibility seriously. And if you have a gift for showing kindness to others, do it gladly." See which of these gifts seem suited to you. Your gifts won't be things that are cumbersome or difficult for you; you should have a tendency to certain actions and duties. And don't think that your gift must be some grand public performance—showing kindness or being an encourager may be almost invisible to the world while making a huge life-changing impact on the person who receives them.

And you probably have more than one spiritual gift. Here's more that Paul writes, and I don't believe it is an exhaustive list, meaning there are more gifts than these:

"There are different kinds of spiritual gifts, but the same Spirit is the source of them all. There are different kinds of service, but we serve the same Lord. God works in different ways, but it is the same God who does the work in all of us. A spiritual gift is given to each of us so we can help each other. To one person the Spirit gives the ability to give wise advice; to another the same Spirit gives a message of special knowledge. The same Spirit gives great faith to another, and to someone else the one Spirit gives the gift of healing. He gives one person the power to perform miracles, and another the ability to prophesy. He gives someone else the ability to discern whether a message is from the Spirit of God or from another spirit. Still another person is given the ability to speak in unknown languages, while another is given the ability to interpret what is being said. It is the one and only Spirit who distributes all these gifts. He alone decides which gift each person should have." (1 Corinthians 12:4-11)

Continue to read God's Word. He will reveal himself to you in more detail and with more application as you get to know him and as he sees your true interest.

Is God a Matchmaker?

Q: I have a question that troubles me a lot. Does God Almighty create a specific woman for a man?

A: I don't believe God picks out a specific woman. I believe you should pray and ask for his guidance in selecting the one who will be your lifelong partner. Use the wisdom that he has given you in his Word. Paul writes that we should not be unequally yoked together with unbelievers, so that is your first guideline: seek a girl who believes in Jesus as her Savior and trusts God with her life, and who is willing to follow him and who understands the biblical role of the husband and wife in marriage.

You can look at the relationships in the Bible and see that no matter who helps or who picks your mate, it will be an ongoing challenge for both of you to love each other and to grow together in God throughout your marriage. Satan doesn't want it to succeed, so you will be fighting: ideally you will be fighting together against the attacks and not against each other as the battle continues over the years. There will be times for each of you when you want to give up, or you don't want to forgive, or you think the grass is greener on the other side of the fence. Determine now to never let those things, those feelings, get the upper hand in your marriage. Be aware now that you will both fail in your commitment; at some point you will question how you could have ever picked her—and she will have her moment thinking of you the same way. It is inevitable because honeymoons don't last for 50, 60, 70 years. So deciding to permanently honor the commitment you will make before God is something you have to do right upfront going into the marriage.

When Eve was created from Adam's rib she was as close to a perfect match as any woman could ever be, and she still failed him; and he failed her by not protecting her from the serpent's tricks—the Scriptures tell us he was standing with her when she sinned and he joined her instead of helping her resist. Abraham and Sarah were married upwards of 100 years and had all kinds of problems. Rebekah was chosen for Isaac by Abraham's servant, having prayed to the Lord for his divine assistance; and that marriage had all kinds of problems.

With sin in the world, there is no perfect mate. But there is a perfect God and he has given us the ability and the power to remain committed to him and to always love and forgive. He modeled it by the way he remains committed to us and always loves and forgives us no matter how many times we fail him. I believe earthly marriage is our opportunity to demonstrate Christlike love and compassion to another human being, reflecting the union of God the Father, God the Son, and God the Holy Spirit. They are one and we, as a married couple, become "one flesh" joined together by God and never to be separated. The fact that much of the world completely fails is not a reflection on him, but a consequence of a growing weakness in the world of a desire for instant gratification, a sense of entitlement as if we deserve better when we are no better.

Can you be like Jesus? Can you love when you're being spit on or beaten or rejected? That is the question, because it will happen. Maybe not literally, although all of those things could literally happen to you. But what will you do when the crisis comes? Can you or will you love when you are receiving no love? That is what will test your spirit and your ability to trust the Holy Spirit. Marriage is not for weaklings. In your search, look for a woman who is serious about the challenges and is willing to go the distance. It will narrow the field because there aren't many men or women thinking hard and long about it.

How to get close to God

Q: I'm trying to get closer to God but every time I do I feel like I'm blocking myself. Do you maybe know what I can do to relinquish all of my control and live a life that's focused on God?

A: The easy answer is: Obedience. Many people want to continue to live in sin but still expect God to bless them and give them peace. It doesn't work. A story I like to share that shows the clear connection is from the Old Testament.

"But Samuel replied, 'What is more pleasing to the Lord: your burnt offerings and sacrifices or your obedience to his voice? Listen! Obedience is better than sacrifice, and submission is better than offering the fat of rams.'" (1 Samuel 15:22)

King Saul had been told to go to war with a wicked idol-worshiping nation and destroy everything, including all of the animals. Instead he decided to keep the best sheep and cattle for himself and his troops. The Lord was furious with him and decided to remove him from his position as king. The verse above is from the prophet Samuel, who was the king's spiritual adviser and the one who spoke for God. Saul had made excuses saying he intended to offer some of his plunder as a sacrifice to the Lord, trying to cover for his greed and disobedience by giving a big offering at church (that's what we would call it today if the same kind of thing happened).

Anytime we don't feel peace from God it's tied directly to disobedience. Even in the middle of terrible conflict, if we're being obedient to God he will give us peace. So the question is what in your life is not glorifying to God? What is an act of disobedience? It might not be something you're doing, but something you're not doing. A suggestion or example would be some slight grudge that you may be holding against someone, refusing to forgive them for something they did or how they hurt you in some way. God forgives us for sinning against him, which is much worse than anything another person could do to us, so it's our responsibility as Christians to forgive. In Genesis it tells us we were created in his image. That means we are supposed to start acting like him.

Another option or way to find a clue to the discomfort you're feeling is to think about what makes you angry or upset. Those are things that need dealt with. God tells us to love our enemies. He places challenges in our lives to test our faith and grow us. Like weight training we need resistance to get bigger spiritual muscles. But if we are living opposed to God's plan for us we will always feel unsettled.

I said that obedience is the easy answer. But it's hard to do if we choose to hang on to our right to be offended. So the answer is easy but doing it is hard. Obedience is better than sacrifice: Jesus had to sacrifice his life on the cross because of our disobedience. It's better to obey.

Liturgical prayers

Q: Is it okay, or not okay, to take a prewritten prayer and use it? Sometimes I feel I say the same things, in the same way, with the same tone, etc. I want to learn how to be more spontaneous and passionate and verbose. I want to learn how to pray the right way, all the time. I seem to trip over my words. I feel embarrassed by a lack of eloquence.

A: I can't think of any prayer that is wrong. As a father I always want to hear from my children, and God made us to be like him so I believe he is the same as a Father to us. As far as types of prayer, I think a prewritten prayer is okay for the purposes of modeling and forming a pattern or schedule of prayer. Jesus gave his disciples the Lord's Prayer in Matthew 6; it's a comprehensive prayer of remembering God, others, and self, and although it starts with "Pray like this:" I don't believe it was supposed to be a substitute for open dialogue with God.

There are some people who like to recite the 23rd Psalm and there's nothing wrong with that; it is very poetic and comforting. Some people pray before meals, some pray in the morning, some pray before going to bed. Some say they pray all day as they try to live in a constant attitude of respect before the Lord. I don't believe he will reject any form of communication.

Psalms 37:4 says, "Take delight in the Lord, and he will give you your heart's desires." Your heart's desires don't follow a pattern since everyone is different and has different desires, so there's no model or prewritten prayer that would fit that verse, which would indicate he wants your own unique heart's desires to be discussed when you talk to him. I'll just encourage you that tripping over your words with him is better than not saying any words at all because, unlike the experiences we sometimes have with our kids, God always understands what we mean.

"And the Holy Spirit helps us in our weakness. For example, we don't know what God wants us to pray for. But the Holy

Spirit prays for us with groanings that cannot be expressed in words. And the Father who knows all hearts knows what the Spirit is saying, for the Spirit pleads for us believers in harmony with God's own will." (Romans 8:26-27)

Bottom line, I think a prewritten prayer is a good idea for helping to develop a habit of prayer. The regular connection with God will cause your prayer life to grow into a more robust, intimate, and personal dialogue as you both get to know each other better through time and intensity.

Did Jesus go to hell?

Q: I've been in search of a scripture for hours now and nobody can help. Scripture where Jesus goes into hell for three days and takes the keys of death, hell, and the grave. Somebody asked and someone else told her the Bible was rewritten and it's all a lot of hogwash. I just want to give her scripture. Please, thanks!

A: It's an interesting question and I hope I can get close to what you're trying to find.

There isn't a place that specifically says Jesus went to hell for three days. Many have taken different passages and formed that opinion but I think it may be in error. See the following:

"For as Jonah was in the belly of the great fish for three days and three nights, so will the Son of Man be in the heart of the earth for three days and three nights." (Matthew 12:40)

"Christ suffered for our sins once for all time. He never sinned, but he died for sinners to bring you safely home to God. He suffered physical death, but he was raised to life in the Spirit. So he went and preached to the spirits in prison—those who disobeyed God long ago when God waited patiently while Noah was building his boat." (1 Peter 3:18-20a)

"I am the living one. I died, but look—I am alive forever and ever! And I hold the keys of death and the grave." (Revelation 1:18, some translations add "and Hades.")

After the crucifixion Jesus was buried in the tomb of Joseph of Arimathea from Friday night until Sunday morning; that's three calendar days "in the heart of the earth."

I don't believe you can take the statement that he "preached to the spirits in prison" and draw the conclusion that he went to hell. We don't know enough about the spiritual world to make that claim and this passage does not clearly say so. Jesus existed before he came here from heaven; he reached out to the lost people in Noah's day just like he does now, in the Spirit, and the lost are certainly captives to sin, so in effect a prison.

When Jesus says he "holds the keys" he didn't have to go there to get them—he has conquered sin and death by his sacrifice on the cross and controls the outcome of our decisions to accept or reject him, and he can do that from his throne in heaven. For a real world example, compare it to your employer holding the keys to your chance of a promotion. I believe these words from Jesus are more allegorical than literal, much like his parables were used to help us understand matters that are beyond our reach.

"Then the King will turn to those on the left and say, 'Away with you, you cursed ones, into the eternal fire prepared for the devil and his demons.'" (Matthew 25:41)

I can't imagine any reason why Jesus would visit hell. Jesus is God. He was there when Satan was cast down from heaven. He knows who is in hell and why. People in hell aren't given a second chance or an opportunity to get out, as illustrated by the parable he told in Luke 16:19-31 in which a rich man who had died and gone to hell was pleading for a beggar in heaven to bring him a drop of water to cool his tongue. The point of the story is that if you won't believe those who God has sent from the living, you won't believe if he sends someone from the dead. Notice that Jesus didn't preach to the lost after he was raised from the dead—he met only with his followers and then ascended to heaven in their presence commanding them to go out and preach the Gospel.

I'm not sure why someone would want to paint a picture of Jesus journeying to hell. To what end?

My life is worse as a Christian

Q: My life is not good at all. There is nothing moving in my life: health, career, financially, spiritually. I have done everything as a Christian but nothing is working out. I used to do what the world is doing, ungodly activities, sexual sin. I leave everything and repent but I don't see any change and now life is worse than before I became a Christian.

A: Christianity saves you from the penalty of sin, which is eternal death and separation from God. But it does not remove sin from the world or all the bad effects that sin has on us and the people and world around us. People will still have financial problems, face discouragement, get sick and hurt and murdered. Total perfection and joy and peace will only come once Jesus returns or God calls us home to himself.

Jesus promised this: "I am leaving you with a gift—peace of mind and heart. And the peace I give is a gift the world cannot give. So don't be troubled or afraid" (John 14:27). But he also said this: "Here on earth you will have many trials and sorrows. But take heart, because I have overcome the world" (John 16:33). He recognized that all will not go smoothly on this side of the fence, but it is temporary.

It sounds like you have a lot of troubles, but you can still have peace. Being a follower of Christ means doing what he does. Love those who persecute you. Care for those who you are able to care for. Work hard at whatever task you are given. Forgive those who wrong you. There is nothing easy about being a Christian. The huge benefit—other than the obvious facts of being forgiven your sins, forgoing the punishment that would have come with them, and being granted eternity with Jesus in heaven and a completely new whole and healed life—is the knowledge that all of this present trouble will not last forever. The lost don't have anything good to look forward to and can only find little bits of happiness in what they can grab and hold onto now, which is extremely limited and fleeting and can be easily taken away from them.

"That is why we never give up. Though our bodies are dying, our spirits are being renewed every day. For our present troubles are small and won't last very long. Yet they produce for us a glory that vastly outweighs them and will last forever! So we don't look at the troubles we can see now; rather, we fix our gaze on things that cannot be seen. For the things we see now will soon be gone, but the things we cannot see will last forever." (2 Corinthians 4:16-18)

How to Forgive

Q: I struggle to forgive.

A: You are not alone. Let's dig deeper into this remarkable gift that we've been given by God.

"If you forgive anyone's sins, they are forgiven. If you do not forgive them, they are not forgiven." (John 20:23)

It is possible that you don't recognize the power you have. Understand what Jesus is saying here: You can forgive sins. In the Gospels there is the story of a paralyzed man being lowered through the ceiling by his friends to be healed by Jesus. The religious leaders who were present criticized Jesus for saying he could forgive sins as well as make the man walk again; "What is he saying? This is blasphemy! Only God can forgive sins!" Jesus did both, but before doing so he replied, "I will prove to you that the Son of Man has the authority on earth to forgive sins." (Mark 2:1-12)

Jesus passed this power to the other "sons" of God; you are not deity, but you are a child of God if you have trusted in the death and resurrection of Jesus as payment for your sins and your hope for eternal life in heaven. He said in John 14, "I tell you the truth, anyone who believes in me will do the same works I have done, and even greater works, because I am going to be with the Father. You can ask for anything in my name, and I will do it, so that the Son can bring glory to the Father."

This is not the same as God forgiving people of sins against himself, but it is you forgiving sins that have been committed against you. Compare it to a courtroom in which two parties are engaged in a legal battle. If the person filing the complaint drops the charges, that case is closed. God will not hold against your enemy a sin that you have forgiven. This is significant because the list of charges is only growing longer as the days wear on.

In Luke 17, Jesus hinted of the immeasurable wrath God reserves for people who harm his children when he declared, "It would be better to be thrown into the sea with a millstone hung around your neck." Jesus, unlike anyone else, knows exactly what is in store for unrepentant and unforgiven sinners. He wants to prevent that cataclysmic ending at any cost, even the cost of his own life. This is what we are called to do when he commands us to forgive others. We are joining him in the battle to save souls.

Your "authority on earth to forgive sins" may lead the one being forgiven to contemplate forgiveness on a greater scale, the forgiveness of sins he or she has committed against one who is much greater than you. The Scriptures say that God is drawing all men to himself and that he doesn't want any to perish. This friction in your relationship, this moment of you offering forgiveness to someone for a very real and painful sin that was committed against you, could be a weakening in the fabric of their resistance to God's grace and mercy. The Temple curtain that ripped when Jesus was crucified allowed us to come directly to God without anyone standing in the way. It happened at the pinnacle of history when love and hate met at the cross. Your ability to forgive, to not hold a sin against someone, could be the Calvary moment that opens the door to their eternity.

Fasting

Q: I want a push. Push me. Fasting is my lifestyle but I am bound in some areas. I can't break through in certain realms of power and glory.

A: Well, I don't know enough about you, but I will start at the beginning. So many people who correspond with me are living just like the rest of the world; it's no wonder they are dissatisfied and unhappy. And these are people who call themselves Christians. So buckle up.

You need to be obedient. Fasting is the practice of denying yourself something, usually food, in order to dedicate that time and energy to praying and meditating and listening to God. Fasting can be good and the Bible records Jesus doing it quite frequently, but it's worthless if you don't obey what the Father tells you to do. There are two primary violations I'm seeing by Christians: promiscuity—they're having sexual relations outside of a marriage commitment—and financial irresponsibility—for a Christian being financially responsible means honoring God first with your monetary resources and then every other financial obligation or wish comes second. Ultimately they are ending up with bad relationships and broke or deeply in debt. Big surprise.

Let me share this verse because some claim to obey but their hearts betray their stated intentions: "What good is fasting when you keep on fighting and quarreling? This kind of fasting will never get you anywhere with me" (Isaiah 58:4). In this passage God was speaking to how the people were mistreating each other, but it can certainly be applied here. I believe more arguments are caused by sex and money than all other problems combined.

Fasting is not a form of worship if it doesn't result in worship. It disgusts God when his people mock him. How do we mock God? In nearly everything we do. We put our offerings in the plate on Sunday and rob our employers of time and attention on Monday. We sing praise songs one minute and curse our neighbor the next. We demand fair treatment from the government but cheat on our taxes. Our words and our actions don't match. Going hungry for a day or two doesn't matter if we starve God of the true praise and worship he is due.

If there is going to be any hope of a closer relationship with the Heavenly Father it must start with an honest evaluation of our personal commitment to him. Disobedience—sin—is a "stench in his nostrils" and he turns his face away from us.

Instead of public declarations of our beliefs, or even private rituals, how about simple proof of them in our acts of service to others—starting with our families and in our homes? Nothing can take the place of an authentic relationship.

And if you don't obey, he won't bless you.

Is it ever too late for Jesus to care?

Q: When is it too late for Jesus to care?

A: It's never too late.

Some time ago I had lunch with a pastor friend. It had been quite a while since our last meeting so we spent a few hours catching up. I shared how I'd been given the opportunity to speak on several Sundays at one of the local retirement homes. He commented that my time might be better used if I were more involved with some of the youth we both knew, that there's not much likelihood of moving the hearts and minds of older people —that they're pretty much set in their ways.

Modern research supports this; there are volumes of surveys and polls by various groups indicating that after the age of about 14 the chances of someone coming to Christ are almost zero.

Then I got a request that same evening asking me if I could fill in again as guest speaker at the retirement home. Curious timing. I accepted, and as I searched for a relevant message what I found was Jesus talking to old people—a lot of them.

"'What do you mean?' exclaimed Nicodemus. 'How can an old man go back into his mother's womb and be born again?' Jesus replied, 'I assure you, no one can enter the Kingdom of God without being born of water and the Spirit.'" (John 3:4-5)

Nicodemus was an elder, a Pharisee, a teacher, a leader of the people; but he came to inquire of Jesus about some of the most serious matters—life-changing matters. Jesus answered all of his questions and much more.

"Soon a Samaritan woman came to draw water, and Jesus said to her, 'Please give me a drink.' He was alone at the time because his disciples had gone into the village to buy some food. The woman was surprised, for Jews refuse to have anything to do with Samaritans. She said to Jesus, 'You are a Jew, and I am a Samaritan woman. Why are you asking me for a drink?' Jesus replied, 'If you only knew the gift God has for you and who you are speaking to, you would ask me, and I would give you living water.'" (John 4:7-10)

No spring chicken or blushing bride, this Samaritan woman had been married five times and was now living with another man to whom she wasn't married. But she needed Jesus and he cared about her.

"One of the criminals hanging beside him scoffed, 'So you're the Messiah, are you? Prove it by saving yourself—and us, too, while you're at it!' But the other criminal protested, 'Don't you fear God even when you have been sentenced to die? We deserve to die for our crimes, but this man hasn't done anything wrong.' Then he said, 'Jesus, remember me when you come into your Kingdom.' And Jesus replied, 'I assure you, today you will be with me in paradise.'" (Luke 23:39-43)

This criminal was certainly no child. He was a grown man, experienced in the ways of the world, hardened to goodness and softness. Forgiveness? He knew he didn't deserve it. But in Jesus he saw hope!

Think of Abraham, Moses, Jeremiah, Hosea, and many others; Joseph and Mary, Zechariah and Elizabeth, the disciples of Jesus. God reached out to all of them, regardless of age or affiliation and none were small children or even youths. He used Jesus or the message of Jesus, and he used prophets and priests, fishermen and tax collectors, and now he wants to use you.

"One day some parents brought their little children to Jesus so he could touch and bless them. But when the disciples saw this, they scolded the parents for bothering him. Then Jesus called for the children and said to the disciples, 'Let the children come to me. Don't stop them! For the Kingdom of God belongs to those who are like these children. I tell you the truth, anyone who doesn't receive the Kingdom of God like a child will never enter it.'" (Luke 18:15-17)

We are all children in relation to the Father, and that will never change regardless of the date on the calendar or the clock on the wall. He is striving to draw us to himself, to make righteous the unrighteous, and to create light where there is darkness. It's never too late and Jesus always cares. You don't need to be a child to come as a child.

The Trinity

Q: Can you please help me understand about the trinity?

A: The word "trinity" isn't in the Bible. It is a word the church uses to represent the single entity that includes God the Father, God the Son, and God the Holy Spirit—in some circles the term used is Godhead. Part of the answer is that no one really understands God completely because he is God and we are humans with a limited capacity to know him, so we struggle to identify or describe him. I'm not so sure that we will even know him completely in heaven because those distinctions will remain, but eternity will certainly allow us the time to discover more and more of him; we won't be blinded by sin like we are now, and the effects of it on our hearts and minds will be removed.

God lives in heaven. In the book of Genesis you will read about God, the Creator, as he forms the world and you will read about the Lord, in the flesh, walking with Adam and Eve in the Garden of Eden. I believe these are manifestations of God the Father and God the Son. Sin is what caused us to no longer see either one because we were kicked out of the Garden; until Jesus was born in Bethlehem. He was the Messiah predicted by scores of prophets and wise men, and he is God the Son—God in the flesh again. When he was crucified and ascended to heaven, he told those present that he would send the Advocate, or Counselor, who is God the Holy Spirit; he will live in us, which is better than just living with us.

All three are the same God, just in different forms based on what he's trying to do with us, for us, and through us. To me, this shows an incredibly loving God who uses as many ways as possible to reach his Creation in an attempt to reconcile us back into a good and right relationship with himself. He didn't create us in our amazing bodies and minds, and in his image, to write us off because of sin. He provided a remedy for sin in the way of Jesus on the cross; he paid the death price that we owed, and that's why we call him Savior. The Holy Spirit that we are granted upon salvation—which means confessing our need of Jesus and trusting him to stand before God on our behalf—is who helps us to discern the will of God here and it's how we can communicate with God in heaven through prayer.

I look at Jesus as the filter through which God sees us now. Sin—which, very simply, is defined as disobedience and rebellion—is so detestable to God that he wouldn't be able to have any relationship with us at all if we remained in our sinful state. You will read elsewhere in Scripture that a third of the angels were cast from heaven when Lucifer sinned and led a rebellion against God. He won't stand for sin of any kind, anywhere. With Jesus we have a pathway to heaven, and with the Holy Spirit we have training in holiness. Hebrews 10:14 says about the sacrifice of Jesus on the cross, "For by that one offering he forever made perfect those who are being made holy." This is our process and work as long as we live, to continue in growth, inviting others to join us, and to patiently wait on our glorious reunion with God. That time is either at the end of this life or when Jesus returns to gather those who haven't yet died. Either way, we end up with God—in his entirety—in heaven forever.

Abortion: Part 1

Q: I have a deep question and need an answer from an outside source that knows the Bible better than me. I just got into a very heated discussion about abortion, miscarriages, and stillbirth. Specifically, what is considered murder, what is wrong, and what constitutes a baby. Could you shed some light on this for me?

A: The first question in any important discussion is whether the participants believe in God's Word. If one or more don't believe the Bible is the complete authority, there is no point in arguing, or even debating, because you aren't on level ground. I offer only biblical counsel because it's the one thing that is reliable and always remains the same throughout the ages. My personal opinions don't matter. And I don't have to win an argument because it's not me who judges—it is really freeing to not have to fight. Anyone can pick whatever side of an argument they want, I stand on what God says and it's up to the listener or reader to believe or disbelieve, to accept or reject.

The Lord told Jeremiah, "I knew you before I formed you in your mother's womb. Before you were born I set you apart and appointed you as my prophet to the nations." This would indicate that human life doesn't have a start date (at conception, 20 weeks, at birth, etc.) but that it is part of a bigger plan that God designed before time began.

Sin impacted the original plan, but it didn't derail God's ultimate plan of life and relationships. With sin comes selfishness, hate, sickness, murder, death. All the forms of ending life are the result of man's sin. As it applies to deaths of unborn babies, miscarriages and stillbirths are due to changes and defects in the body that wouldn't exist if the consequences of sin weren't present. Even complications rooted in the man, such as poor connections between sperm and egg, genetic defects, and so on, are a result of sin and the imperfections it causes.

Abortion is the willful, active taking of a life. It is murder. The Bible says, "Thou shalt not kill." That translates to murder, the taking of innocent life, not to the justice he holds for unrepentant sinners in eternity or even now on earth. The difference is important because God commanded the killing of entire nations who were evil and worshiped idols, and God does not sin; this distinction matters because there must be no contradiction between his commandments and our understanding of them.

Using abortion as a method of birth control is a gory, disgusting abuse of the freedoms God has granted us. The popular view of "My body, My choice" is great as long as there is the realization that it will also include "My consequences when standing before God."

What about the situation of rape or incest that results in pregnancy? As difficult as this may seem, that tiny life is a gift from God; no one else gets to claim responsibility for causing the miracle of life. Is it the baby's fault that people sinned? Is it a tragic and permanent reminder of a violent or unwelcome event in the woman's life? Maybe. But it is also a child, a human being, that only exists because God granted it life—can we ask instead what good is there in it, what blessings can come from it? We need to look at the bigger picture. God knows what he is doing even in the case of a life formed from a sinful act; in fact, even under ideal circumstances, he allows a sinful husband and a sinful wife to produce another sinner. We are all born in sin and need the same Savior, so to take the case of conception under undesirable circumstances to its final conclusion would be to deny any new life at all since it can only ever be the product of two sinners.

What happens to the woman or man in any of these situations who has sinned, who has chosen incorrectly and violated this precious thing God designed called life? Confess it and accept his forgiveness. It is no bigger sin than any other sin because all sin separates us from him; we cannot pretend to be self-righteous and think that someone else's sins are worse than ours or that we are better than anyone else. We are all sinners. God is merciful to sinners.

Abortion: Part 2

I received a woman's letter expressing an almost debilitating fear of seeing her aborted baby in heaven. She was terrified of what this child would think of her. I want to share the thoughts I gave her, in the hopes that it may help some of you, too.

In Revelation 21:5 Jesus, seated on his throne in heaven, tells John to write down these words: "Behold, I make all things new." The very moment that we arrive to meet God, we will have a new understanding. Her baby already understands the horror and pain that sin has caused in the world—it's why Jesus had to come in the first place; he conquered sin and the effects of sin and the consequences of sin.

Heaven will be a place of total forgiveness and restoration, not only by God, but by those we see there who we may have harmed here. And God does not grade sin; man does that. In Acts 10:34 Paul writes, "Now I really understand that God doesn't show favoritism." Aborting a baby or stealing a paperclip at the office are both sins. Sin, period, is what separates us from God's acceptance and approval, and whether that distance is a millimeter or a mile, it's still completely apart from him. That's why: Jesus.

Don't you believe for a minute that any sin you've confessed to God and he's graciously promised to forgive, regardless of its comparative gravity or insignificance, is going to keep you from his smile or the glad welcome of everyone in heaven. Including babies!

The sins of the father

Q: What do you do when all your efforts seem in vain? I pray and involve God in my plans and decisions and it all comes back hurtful. I am surrounded with pain, hate, sickness, unemployment, and abandonment. How do I stand in the storm when all efforts fail, should I stop trying?

A: Hey, don't stop trying. The night Jesus was arrested he prayed to God for another way because he could see the looming pain of the cross. But he resigned himself to following the path set before him whether or not it was painful; honoring God was and is the first priority of a person who is committed to him.

I don't know anything about you, but I do know what I see around the world as a general theme, so I will reply accordingly. If I offend you, I apologize in advance because that is not my goal. I love you as a sister in the Lord and I want the best for you.

If you're not married, you are in a relationship or trying to be in one. I've done a lot of counseling with young people, and almost without exception they are sexually active. This is the beginning of their problems. God requires a holy life and your body is his temple. Sexual activity is for married people, people who have made a lifetime commitment to each other and pledged to honor God and their mate with loyalty and fidelity. This is almost a foreign concept in a world that promotes sex on demand with anyone and without commitment.

When people decide to follow Jesus and then follow their own flesh desires, there is a conflict in their spirits, there is unrest, and there is a lack of blessing from God. You can't be serious about Jesus and casual with your body.

Maybe I'm completely off base and I encourage you to tell me so, but we were created from the very beginning to be in a "one-flesh" relationship and that is why it's the root of so many problems—because we don't honor the way we were made by our Creator.

If this hits home with you, what do you do now? Well, I would ask you to do what you do any time you feel convicted of sin: confess it to God, stop doing it, and determine to move forward honoring him with you body and your mind and your heart and your spirit. He forgives and heals. And obedience is what opens the floodgates of heaven to his blessings on your life.

Q: Wow. Thank you! Yes, I am in a relationship and we are sexual. Is what I am going through the punishment for having sex outside of marriage? Some of the challenges I am facing happened way back before I was born and honestly I am paying the price of a failed marriage. I want to be right with God and I want to be whole.

A: I don't think of our difficulties in life as punishment. Jesus had to go to the cross because of all our stupid choices, so there is no punishment greater than that. I see them as the results of sin, lack of obedience, and refusal to honor God. We live in a fallen world and perfection won't happen until Jesus returns. But that's no excuse to pass up the blessings God wants to pour out on us now. Salvation is a gift, but everything else is extra and he's loaded with things he can give us. But only if we treat our relationship with him more seriously than we usually do. Anything or anyone you set up as more important than him becomes your new god.

Don't use the past as a crutch for why you are where you are. Your parents were and are on their own journey of discovery. God is working in their lives, trying to draw them to himself. They are created beings, just like you and me, and they have the same choices to make, making big messes sometimes. Yes, they affected you, but you have your own choices to make. Look forward, not backward. You can't do anything about them, but you can do everything about you. God is bigger than any problem you face, and he is intimately aware of what you're going through. I can picture him in my mind, waiting patiently to see what you'll do with the options in front of you. Will you choose him, or . . . ?

Q: My father remarried and treats me and my brother like bothers. My step-siblings are given everything from expensive education, cars, and even vacation. We are not given anything, not even a visit to know where home is. At times I feel so alone not having that father figure. It hurts knowing that I didn't choose him but God gave him the responsibility, and from his actions he has failed extremely. How do I forge ahead and not harbor any hate towards him, how do I see myself as God's loved one when I don't experience it here? My mother refused to sue him knowing full well the courts can easily judge in our favor but she stands firmly that God will see us through. It's been twenty years since their divorce and I am awaiting the miracle that he could love us but to no avail.

A: "Don't fret because of evildoers; don't envy the wicked. For evil people have no future; the light of the wicked will be snuffed out." (Proverbs 24:19-20)

The reason we have to pray for those who hurt us is because their end is destruction. At our very root, at the point of being a follower of Christ, we must love who he loves. Does he love what your father has done? Absolutely not, but he doesn't want him lost to hell. So he gives him breath each day, drawing him, trying to get his attention. Your father may have failed miserably, but God used him to create you, and you are his beautiful child, designed for personal greatness and God's own glory. You didn't choose your father, but God chose you. That's better.

Regarding your own wellbeing: do the best you can with what you have. Honor God with your body. Give him your mind and heart. Trust him with your finances. Work as unto the Lord. If you aren't in a job that you love, love the God who allowed you to get it. If you aren't working, find something to do—even volunteering somewhere until you can find a paid position. Be around people who can be a source of work or referrals, or who need to see a light in this dark world. With Jesus, you are that light. Smiles are free.

Your earthly father may never be what you want him to be. But your heavenly Father is more than you can even imagine. He loves you with an everlasting love. Don't focus on what you don't have, but on what you do have. You have an intelligent mind and a unique design. No one is like you; you have special gifts and talents that God gave you alone. Dig deep and discover who you are in his eyes. Your mother is right. God will see you through. He is trustworthy.

Ten months later:

Q: Hey, Timothy. I can't thank you enough for the encouragements you sent to me. From the day I decided to forgive my dad, I have seen doors opening. I forgive him every day because I get to discover hurtful things daily. I have found my self-worth and have built my self-esteem. Whenever I feel low I am reminded of how God loves me so much to even sacrifice his Son, it always encourages me to love back and also to realize that everyone has a battle I may not be aware of. I'm now working, a miraculous job I must say, and I am engaged to be married this November. Thank you so much for encouraging me, a stranger, finding time to talk to me and make me closer to

God. May God bless your family and ministry. With so much love from me. I will keep praying for you!

A: You are amazing! Thanks for the update and all the good news. God is doing something wonderful with you and there is more to come! Love and blessings, Tim.

When do I have to start making disciples?

Q: At what stage in a Christian life is one required to undertake the assignment of making disciples?

A: Very good question! The last command Jesus gave us before ascending into heaven was to go and make disciples of all the nations, and it can seem very intimidating. But remember who he was talking to—followers whose faith he constantly challenged and who weren't schooled in theology or evangelism.

Earlier in his ministry Jesus had sent out the twelve disciples to prepare the way for his message, but also to "heal the sick, raise the dead, cure those with leprosy, and cast out demons." He told them to go without any money or food or even a change of clothes, but to look for a trustworthy person in each town with whom they could stay.

I can imagine the looks of alarm on their faces as they anticipated the kind of reception they would meet and whether they would be able to answer the arguments of those who resisted. They must have been filled with anxiety and doubt because he then told them, "Don't worry about how to respond or what to say. God will give you the right words at the right time." (Matthew 10:19)

When Jesus returned to heaven he sent his Holy Spirit to live in us and guide us in all ways. Later, Peter and John were arrested and called before the religious leaders to explain by what authority they were preaching to the crowds. The passage in Acts records, "The members of the council were amazed when they saw the boldness of Peter and John, for they could see that they were ordinary men with no special training in the Scriptures. They also recognized them as men who had been with Jesus."

Never fear when your opportunity arises. The perfect time to share the hope of your salvation is today. With Jesus you have immeasurably more resources than the person who doesn't have him. So live in such a way that the people you meet will be amazed at your boldness and recognize you as someone who has been with Jesus.

How to get to heaven (according to God)

How to get to heaven:

"But now God has shown us a way to be made right with him without keeping the requirements of the law, as was promised in the writings of Moses and the prophets long ago.

We are made right with God by placing our faith in Jesus Christ. And this is true for everyone who believes, no matter who we are.

For everyone has sinned; we all fall short of God's glorious standard.

Yet God, in his grace, freely makes us right in his sight. He did this through Christ Jesus when he freed us from the penalty for our sins.

For God presented Jesus as the sacrifice for sin. People are made right with God when they believe that Jesus sacrificed his life, shedding his blood. This sacrifice shows that God was being fair when he held back and did not punish those who sinned in times past, for he was looking ahead and including them in what he would do in this present time.

God did this to demonstrate his righteousness, for he himself is fair and just, and he makes sinners right in his sight when they believe in Jesus." (Romans 3:21-26)

No commentary needed.

About the Author

Tim Leiphart is an author and biblical counselor with an international daily devotional blog. A unique history of military service and national leadership in the financial services industry, along with decades of concurrent duties as a guest speaker for churches, a board chaplain for two non-profit organizations, a personal, marriage, and financial counselor, a Bible teacher to all age groups, and a mentor to young adults has positioned him with the life experience and a viewpoint to serve the spiritual and relational development needs of Christians all over the world. His latest books are a result of the dialogue he's enjoyed with his loyal readers. Born in Gettysburg, Pennsylvania, USA, Tim married the love of his life in 1983; they have two grown children and three granddaughters.

The Third Timothy™ brand is a consequence of a meeting with Bible school students in Guatemala. When the translator introduced him, they laughed and said, "Oh, like First and Second Timothy—Third Timothy!" The label fits perfectly with his life priorities of God first, others second, and self third. Recently it's been modified to represent not only the blog and various Christian devotional books, but other future discipleship products intended to make a greater impact on global outreach. "Uniting the Children of God" is the brand motto and mission purpose of international biblical counseling designed to bring believers together, recognize the common struggles of living for God in an increasingly ungodly world, and encourage deeper spiritual growth.

NOTES

NOTES

NOTES

NOTES

NOTES

NOTES

56329512R00064

Made in the USA
Middletown, DE
20 July 2019